GETTING OUT OF DEBT

Money Management: You Cannot Afford To Wait Any Longer

MICHAEL STEVEN

Rich or Poor, 9 Simple Rules to Clear Your Debts Faster, and Rebuild your Credit

© **Copyright 2020 - All rights reserved.**

The content contained within this book may not be reproduced, duplicated, or transmitted without direct written permission from the author or the publisher.

For more information:

Website: VAGPublishing.com

Email: Michael@TheBestSellerBooks.com

Under no circumstances will any blame or legal responsibility be held against the publisher, or author, for any damages, reparation, or monetary loss due to the information contained within this book. Either directly or indirectly. You are responsible for your own choices, actions, and results.

Legal Notice:

This book is copyright protected. This book is only for personal use. You cannot amend, distribute, sell, use, quote or paraphrase any part, or the content within this book, without the consent of the author or publisher.

Disclaimer Notice:

Please note the information contained within this document is for educational purposes only. All effort has been executed to present accurate, up to date, and reliable, complete information. No warranties of any kind are declared or implied. Readers acknowledge that the author is not engaging in the rendering of legal, financial, medical, or professional advice. The content within this book has been derived from various sources. Please consult a licensed professional before attempting any techniques outlined in this book.

By reading this document, the reader agrees that under no circumstances is the author responsible for any losses, direct or indirect, which are incurred as a result of the use of the information contained within this document, including, but not limited to, — errors, omissions, or inaccuracies.

CONTENTS

Financial Freedom Checklist	v
Introduction	vii
Chapter One: How Did We Get Here?	1
Chapter Two: Transforming Your Relationship With Debt	17
Chapter Three: Taking Stock Of Your Current Situation	30
Chapter Four: Tackling Your Debt	45
Chapter Five: Staying Out of Debt	74
Chapter Six: Building Your Wealth	85
Final Words	103
Other Books by Michael Steven	105
Financial Freedom Checklist	107
Additional Resource	108
References	111

FINANCIAL FREEDOM CHECKLIST

(A Simple list that should be followed to the "T")

This checklist includes:

❏ 11 important steps that you should follow to achieve success and head toward *Financial Freedom.*

❏ Plus, bonus advice.

Forget about yesterday and start thinking about tomorrow!

> *"The past and the future are separated by a second,*
> *so make that second count!"*
> —Carmine Pirone

To receive your Financial Freedom With Real Estate checklist, visit the link:

www.thebestsellerbooks.com

INTRODUCTION

"When you get in debt, you become a slave."

– Andrew Jackson

Debt is more than just a weight on your shoulders that causes stress and financial strain; it is a manacle that holds you back from achieving your dreams and becoming the best version of yourself. Think of what you wish to accomplish in life, like starting a business; traveling; relocating to another country; buying your dream car; or buying a home. Debt limits your options because the money you make must go towards settling monthly repayments on time instead of investing in those things you wish to accomplish. You shelve your life goals because they seem implausible when in debt.

This book will dispel common debt misconceptions in order to help you get out of debt, regardless of if you are struggling to make your monthly payments. It helps you understand your current financial standing and how you can incorporate all debt payments without compromising your quality of life. Additionally, it explains in detail how to ensure that you remain debt-free once you get there. We are a debt-driven society where people abide by the notion that a little debt won't hurt, especially when we want something we cannot afford.

It usually starts with small credit card purchases and, before you know it, you have accumulated thousands of dollars in debt. At this point, you may have to forego some non-essential personal treats like attending parties, remodeling your home, or going on vacations, because your income is compromised. Eventually, you begin living paycheck to paycheck as you strive to stay on top of responsibilities and bills. You live in fear that you will run out of cash, or that you will not have enough money to handle your responsibilities, or that you will be taken to court.

Such fear exacts pressure on you whether you realize it or not. It disrupts your life and your personal relationships. It can zap your pleasure and joy until you eventually develop physical and emotional stress. You feel hopeless and defeated because of the constant anxiety and despair. Bottom line? Being in debt can wreak havoc on your life. This book will show you how to make smart money choices that get you out of debt fast and reduce stress by helping you determine how much you need to set aside for debt repayment through practical calculations.

The current total US consumer debt stands at a staggering $14.3 trillion in 2020. Mortgages make up 68% of the debt, but non-housing debts such as auto loans, student loans, and credit card loans continue to increase. This means that almost every US household is in some form of debt, whether it's auto, mortgage, credit card, or student loans. With statistics like these, you may derive comfort in knowing that you are not struggling alone. But, debt affects your personal finances, and it always comes with a price tag in the form of interest. The higher the interest rate and the longer you take to pay it off, the higher your debt load, and the more you compromise your future income.

I work as a mortgage specialist at a top bank, and despite having a six-figure income, it seemed like putting money aside wasn't always an easy thing to do. I later realized that the source of this was from my need to constantly upgrade my lifestyle. With that realization, I adopted new money management techniques and gradually paid off all debts, and eventually started investing in real estate. Now, I teach people how to eliminate debts, build their credit score, and start investing in real estate, just like I did. I've taught thousands of people how to achieve financial freedom by getting out of debt and achieving their most precious dreams.

The material offered in this book is derived from my personal experience with debt and how I overcame it, without taking an overtime job or compromising on responsibilities. Therefore, it is the perfect blueprint for people who feel overwhelmed by debt, do not understand their finances, and are ready to make the tough decisions in order to fully pay off debts and remain debt-free.

However, it is impossible to be a completely debt-free society. Debt is a powerful force that can build the world when used responsibly. For instance, financially savvy people use debt to create more wealth, while the financially unaware use debt to destroy their lives. There are good debts and bad debts. Unfortunately, most people take on bad debts, either because they lack information or have competing priorities in life. As the world's financial sector changes, it is important to learn how to minimize the bad debt and how to responsibly use good debt to help yourself.

The debt problems cut across all social strata from lawyers, doctors, nurses, teachers, business executives, casual workers, and even the unemployed population. The debt amounts may vary based on income level and lifestyle preferences, but its effect on personal finances is constant. Therefore, the tips on how to get out of debt in this book are designed to help everyone, regardless of their career or social status. These are tried-and-true principles that I followed to get out of debt and build a real estate business. I was able to do all this with the same salary that initially I thought could not sustain me.

It is all in the mind! Change your mindset about debt, adopt the recommended personal finance management techniques, and remain dedicated to being debt-free. A lot may be said about how and why you need to get out of debt, but if you do not treat your finances differently, you are bound to be stuck in debt and all the stress that comes with it. Read on and learn how to liberate yourself from debts now and in the future.

CHAPTER ONE: HOW DID WE GET HERE?

Ever looked at your debt and wondered how you got there? Well, you are not alone. Most Americans are in debt and struggling to juggle payments and bills every month. Although the reasons for getting into debt may have been unavoidable (due to unemployment or unforeseen emergencies), most people accumulate debt due to bad spending habits. While we understand that using credit cards excessively or borrowing money when you cannot afford to pay it back causes financial strain in the future, we sometimes overlook that in order to satiate current desires. Moreover, debt has been normalized through the vigorous advertisements that promise to offer immediate financial solutions —"No credit? Poor credit? No problem!" Such advertisements send the wrong message that most Americans, if not all, are in debt with poor credit scores.

Though we take on debt with the confidence that we will pay it off, we know that it can lead to disastrous consequences should we lose our main source of income. Debt can consume all your assets, hurt meaningful relationships, and cause stress. Unfortunately, a good number of people deep in a debt crisis never understand the real cause of it. Therefore, the first step towards getting out of debt is understanding the reasons behind it. Let's take a look at some of these reasons individually.

Reduction of income

If you are in debt, it means that your expenses exceed your monthly income. So what would happen if you were to lose your well-paying job, and you had to settle for a reduced income? Most people uphold the same lifestyle they had when earning a high income. This is a recipe for financial disaster. If you fail to adjust your life to fit your income, you will definitely fall in the debt trap, faster than you can imagine. Always make sure you understand your income changes and create a reasonable budget around it.

Divorce

Unfortunately, more than half of American marriages end in divorce. Divorce, whether mutually agreed upon or not, causes financial strain for both parties. On top of paying costly legal fees, American law dictates what should be done with your money during the divorce settlement. If your partner demands more than you can afford, you will be compelled to go into debt to pay what your partner demands.

Poor money management skills

For most people, poor budgeting and money management lead them to take out loans. Worse yet, without a well laid out budget, you cannot track and monitor your expenses. To start monthly budgeting, write down your expenses for an entire month so you know what you spend money on. This is the best way to determine unnecessary expenses, which will help you manage your money better in order to pay off current debts.

Underemployment

Underemployment is especially common among recent graduates who are willing to settle for the first job offer they receive, as they continue to search for a better paying job. This way, they view underemployment as temporary. However, underemployment can have a lasting effect on their personal finances, especially if they have to borrow money to make ends meet. If you are underemployed, it would help to live within your means as you look for a second job or a better paying job. This eliminates the possibility of falling into the debt trap.

Gambling

Gambling is a popular form of entertainment in America. In reality, it is a guaranteed expense. "The house" always wins. Unfortunately, gambling is an addiction, and gamblers are addicted to the idea of winning big. This addiction could drive them to extreme measures to continue gambling. Some even go to the extent of mortgaging their future to "the house" as they aim to win big. If you really love gambling, it would be wise to have a gambling budget and be disciplined enough not to spend more than you budgeted for.

Medical expenses

Expensive healthcare or health emergencies make medical expenses one of the easiest ways for someone to get into debt.

Every medical procedure or consultation, no matter how minor, costs money. Hospitals and doctors get impatient with people who do not settle their medical expenses on time (Anya). This forces patients who are in need of medical care yet lack the finances to take out loans.

Little or no savings

The best way to avoid debt is by being partly or wholly prepared for unanticipated expenses through savings. However, we rarely think of the future; we typically only think of maintaining the status quo and buying all the things we want. A decent saving comes in handy in times of emergency, like losing your source of income, divorce, or illness. You will never regret saving money for future use or emergencies.

These causes of debt are very common and easy to fall into. But, they can be avoided by learning and developing good personal finance budgeting and management skills. It is important to live within your financial means in order to avoid accruing debts.

Consumer debt statistics and impact

Consumer debt consists of personal debts that are incurred as a result of purchasing things that are used for individual or household consumption. Student loans, mortgages, auto loans, payday loans, and credit card debt are examples of consumer debt. This type of debt is in contrast with debts that are incurred through government operations or for use in investments like running a business. Consumer debts are extended by credit unions, banks, or the federal government. Consumer loans are divided into two categories; revolving and non-revolving debts. Revolving debts are debts that are paid monthly, like credit cards, while non-revolving debts are upfront lump sum loans with fixed repayment amounts over a predetermined period, like student and auto loans.

Consumer loans are dubbed trivial means of financing because they attract extremely high interest rates. Moreover, consumer items like clothes, jewelry, and electronics that are purchased using credit cards barely provide necessary utility and depreciate in value with time. But, there is a caveat to consumer debts; increased consumer spending triggers economic growth. For example, people borrow money for housing or education during their early life stages and pay off debts later when they secure higher-paying jobs. Student loans are considered a means to an end because education paves the way for better and higher-paying jobs. These jobs create a positive trajectory for both the economy and the individual.

Regardless of whether some consumer debts are beneficial, they always compromise your financial stability. The United States consumer debt is on the rise owing to ease of obtaining loans that are matched with very high interest rates. According to the latest report released in March 2020, the US consumer debt stood at $4.21 trillion. Non-revolving debt accounted for $3.14 trillion, a rise of about 6% from the previous month. A large percentage of this non-revolving debt was auto loans and student loans. Student loans stood at $1.68 trillion and auto loans at $1.19 trillion. Credit card loans were $1.07 trillion while mortgage balances accounted for $9.71 trillion. This paints a clear picture of the types of debt Americans acquire and helps to explain the spending patterns and reasons people get into debt.

Consumer debt statistics are a clear indication that we live in a debt prone society. Traditional economic theories suggest that people incur debts and manage their finances based on their speculations of future earnings. For instance, debts are mainly acquired during young adulthood, when income is low but the cost of housing and education is high. The borrowing trend tends to reduce as people approach middle age and gradually die down as we continue to age. This implies that life stages and age determine borrowing patterns. However, this theory is gradually changing since the ability to borrow money not only depends on credit history and age, but also on demographic characteristics and macroeconomics. Debt accumulation is greatly influenced by sociological factors like consumerism; the notion that a person's happiness and well-being depends on their ability to purchase consumer goods. Society identifies consumption as the main element of social identity. This drives people to adopt a status-enhancing consumption that is only possible through borrowing and accumulation of unnecessary debts.

The growth of auto loans and student loans has changed the composition of the household and aggregate debt and has made households less effective at supporting wealth accumulation. Conversely, the number of retirees with debts has been on the rise. Also, the debt burden tends to be higher in middle-income households. Below-average income households are recording low debt levels from unsecured loans, unpaid bills, and credit cards. Though borrowing is the conventional path to debt accumulation, households facing emergencies, income shock, or the inability to make ends meet tend to incur expenses that eventually drive them into debt without necessarily borrowing money. Some people may be unaware of such debts until a debt collection agency calls or the information reflects on their credit report. The main causes of non-loan debts are local government or state fees and fines, unpaid bills, and out-of-pocket medical bills.

Consumer debt can be a positive force because it supports economic growth; however, it bears negative, serious, and widespread impacts on affected households. It is the main cause of financial distress when household incomes are barely adequate to service the high (and rising) debt burdens. Carrying too much debt creates a downward spiral that begins with higher costs of debt and may lead to court or garnishment of tax refunds and wages. The ultimate consequence of incurring too much debt is bankruptcy and failure to build wealth. Building wealth as a young adult is especially relevant because as you age your ability to save and invest towards the future is compromised.

The credit and debt pathways that lead to mobility are becoming unreliable and broken for borrowers. For example, the high student loan levels have raised concerns on whether the benefits of a degree outweigh the costs to attain it, given their role in entrenching racial wealth inequality and reducing homeownership. Other negative impacts of consumer debt that are not factored in balance sheets include mental and physical health challenges. As aforementioned, debt affects personal relationships whether with family members, your partner, or friends.

DRIVERS OF CONSUMER DEBT

The main drivers of consumer debt are economic, psychological, and cultural, particularly characteristics like age and income. These drivers affect the type and amount of debt incurred by individuals and families. The traditional viewpoint of debt is that households and individuals act rationally with regard to debt accumulation and management. This viewpoint is based on the expectations of future income. Often, people do not like the spending constraints that are tied to current income, because they feel it isn't sufficient to cover their current needs. As such, they opt to borrow money to meet their needs and attain a certain standard of living.

The life cycle hypothesis and the permanent income hypothesis theories explain how and why individuals save and get into debt as a way of ensuring smooth consumption. The two theories predict that individuals and households borrow more during young adulthood when they do not have adequate financial resources to cover the cost of their education and housing needs and pay down the debts as they age. A research study conducted in 2017 of Americans born between 1915 and 1924 ascertained the two theories; their debts increased steadily up to the age of 45 years and began falling in the following years (The aspen institute, 2018). This is attributed to the fact that they were earning a higher income and had less major financial obligations.

However, the two theories do not explain the major aspects of consumer saving, debt accumulation, and repayment patterns. This is because consumers are now borrowing and consuming less in early adulthood than the theories predict, yet consume and borrow more during middle age. As a result, Americans are carrying debt to their retirement years, where they rely on a fixed income. Additionally, it appears the theories fail to account for the increased number of multi-generational households and late-life household formations.

The changing economic nature also diverges from the theories. The theories view income and financial shock as isolated events yet income volatility is a chronic problem among workers. Debt that seems reasonable and rational on the onset becomes a problem due to unaffordability in the long run as a result of volatility shock. Additionally, as income becomes more volatile, it also stagnates. For instance, there is a decreasing median income trend among men (The aspen institute, 2018).

Macroeconomic drivers

Credit supply and business cycles play a major role in the rise of consumer debt. This is because the availability of credit when the economy is thriving contributes to increased consumer debts and vice versa during times of recession. Moreover, credit utilization rates remain constant through business cycles as borrowers are sensitive to credit limits. As such, when consumers are granted access to more credit, their debt levels increase proportionately and when access to credit reduces, their debts reduce proportionally. Since the great recession, the increase in the cost of food, housing, and healthcare have been disproportionate to the increase in individual and household incomes. The increasing cost of living and essential services has been difficult for most individuals and households to avoid. Therefore, they rely on debts to meet their consumption requirements as they struggle to cope with stagnating incomes and rising costs of living. Notably, households that struggle financially get into debt to make ends meet, while financially secure households borrow to maintain a certain standard of living. In both scenarios, borrowing to meet current needs undermines future financial security by reducing disposable income and cutting down on savings.

Availability of credit

The driving force behind rising consumer debt is access to credit. The availability of credit determines the type and amount of debt consumers incur both in the short- and long-term. Moreover, access to credit is determined by an individual's financial position, like their previous debt repayment patterns, or factors beyond their control, like the supply of credit in a current economy. However, the core determinant of credit access is a borrower's financial status, credit use history, and payment of debts. Secured loans rely on asset and income information for underwriting purposes while unsecured loans rely on income and bank account history.

In regard to a borrower's financial history, the types of past debts and timeliness of repayments are key determinants of whether a lender can extend credit to them. But, it is just one factor among many that creditors consider when determining the amount of credit to offer and its cost. Other factors that creditors consider include; cash flow or income level, time of residency in America, and age. In retrospect, recent immigrants and young adults are likely to attract higher interest rates, or unable to get credit because the credit report years and data are core determinants of an individual's credit score. Predominantly, credit availability and access are tied to financial inequality where low-income households have better credit access and tend to pay less for the debts as compared to high-income inequality regions (Kyoung et al, 2017). On the contrary, low-income households with negative asset net worth have limited access to credit, a factor that reinforces their future borrowing abilities but hampers their ability to maintain smooth consumption (Kyoung et al, 2017). Younger adults with low income and net worth have limited access to mainstream and affordable credit. This drives them to opt for informal and high-cost loan alternatives, but some opt to forego borrowing, which in turn limits their ability to amass assets. Conversely, people with high incomes and more wealth have better credit access and as a result, they accumulate debt to either maintain certain living standards or build more wealth.

Consumer culture

The rising debt crisis is attributed to the changing tide of consumerism in America. According to the United States Department of Labor, average spending among individuals increased by more than 12% between the years 2012 and 2016. Further, it revealed that Americans spend more money on restaurants as compared to groceries, and shopping is a favorite pastime. The constantly increasing consumerism is fueled by sociological factors that trigger households to borrow and spend irrationally. To an extent, consumption and spending can be linked to social identity. People get into debt because they want to maintain a certain social status, often without considering its economic sustainability. Status competition drives people to prefer the appearance of wealth over the accumulation of actual wealth. Conversely, social pressures linked with the perception that expensive higher education is better drives students to acquire more expensive student loans for elite higher education.

The consumer culture encourages spending and borrowing, but social norms determine the nature of debts. Hence, debt is classified into two categories; bad debt and good debt. The two debt concepts have very powerful decision-making influence when taking out debt. Good debts increase an individual's net worth and value in the future. Examples of good debt are student loans, business loans, and mortgage loans. On the other hand, bad debts are high-cost and unsecured loans like credit card loans and payday loans. Whether a debt is good or bad depends on its context. For instance, in as much as student loans are classified as good debts, the degree of benefit to the borrower varies based on factors that are beyond their control, such as economic performance, availability of employment upon graduation, and interest rates. In light of this, bad debts can also have positive outcomes in the long run. Strategic use of credit cards can offer benefits like improved credit scores, which later grant access to better credit facilities that can be used to create wealth.

A consumer's interpretation of debt as either good or bad influences their borrowing patterns, asset ownership, and ability to build wealth. Attitude towards debt determines a household's level of debt in that those that view debt as good are more likely to have more loans. Though Americans are eager to take out debt as a means of facilitating smooth consumption, it is a burden to many. This is because most people take out debt to live beyond their means.

Bad Debt and Why You Should Avoid It

Bad debts are debts that are taken out to purchase items that do not generate long-term income and lose value quickly. Debts that attract high interest rates are also classified as bad debts.

Credit card loans

A credit card is issued by financial institutions to their customers to enable them to purchase items and services on credit and repay later with interest. The repayment of used funds might attract other charges that have been agreed upon by both the cardholder and the financial institution. Some financial institutions that issue credit cards give the cardholders an opportunity to borrow money in cash. There is usually a set limit for the amount an individual can borrow that is dependent on the creditor's rating. A good number of people use this method as their preferred mode of paying for goods and services.

Credits cards can put you in a very unhealthy state financially due to the high rates of interest that they attract. Credit companies impose a high-interest rate for their loans, so if a lot of debt was accrued for a long time, the consumer might end up struggling with repayments. In fact, buying goods or services using credit cards is more or less the same as using the higher purchases to procure your preferred items. Let's look at an example. Assuming you purchase a 50-inch flat-screen TV for $1200 using your credit card with an interest rate of 18.9% and decide to repay $60 per month, it would take you around 20 months to fully repay the debt. The total amount paid will have increased to $1,696. $496.47 is a huge amount to pay as interest if you are keen on personal finance management.

In a recent study by Nerdwallet, they found that an average household has debt of around $1600. While the credit utilization is set to 30%, that means most people are above the credit utilization ratio. The usage of a higher credit utilization ratio may affect the cardholder's credit score, translating to higher rates once they apply for new loans or credit. Compared to other forms of loans, credit cards have proven to be the most expensive during reimbursement. Credit cards are referred to as bad debt because they are loans that will end up killing your financial goals. These are debts that can be avoided, yet most Americans rely on them to cater to their daily wants and needs.

The law authorizes credit card issuers to allow a grace period of 21 days before they impose interest on any purchase made. Consumers should consider repaying the debts during this period to avoid additional costs on their purchases. Credit card users should repay their debts on time to improve their credit score and stand a chance of obtaining financing from other institutions.

Payday loans

A payday loan is a type of credit that is given alongside your salary. This loan is short term since its reimbursement period can be as short as two weeks. Payday loans are available online as well as through traditional means of going to a physical financier. These loans are created to serve people who need cash in an emergency situation since the application process is very fast. Lenders verify income and their bank checking account in order to determine the creditor's capability to repay. Once they have approved the loan eligibility, they deposit the money to your account. The creditor is then supposed to write them a postdated check of the total amount borrowed plus the interest with the agreed date of payment. The postdated check acts as collateral since they don't want to follow up on repayments.

Sometimes people are forced to take out payday loans because they have no access to any other emergency credit line. They opt to take the risk of dealing with predatory payday lenders out of necessity. The other category of people that procure this type of loan is those with zero savings. According to a 2019 survey by Go Banking Rates, at least 69% of American households had savings below $1000. This survey explains why payday loan lenders have a ripe market in the US. Pew Charitable trust says that at least 12 million Americans borrow payday loans annually and end up accruing $9 billion in interest charges. That's one reason why federal lawmakers are considering a reduction of interest from 400% to 36% (Megan, 2019).

Most people in the US survive paycheck to paycheck (Zack, 2019). While payday loans are typically used for emergencies, a lot of people use them for daily expenses. This is attributed to their poor spending and borrowing patterns. Once a debtor receives their monthly income and a portion of it is used to repay the loan, it creates a need for another and the vicious cycle continues each month.

Payday loans come in handy in times of emergencies or other unanticipated financial needs. However, they should be avoided. They charge extremely high interest rates and compromise your ability to get through the month without having to take on additional debt to cover your bills. Moreover, payday loans are limited to amounts below $1000 because they are governed by stringent repayment policies. Meaning that unless a debtor has a very high income, it would be almost impossible to offset a $1000 loan using a single paycheck. Payday loan lenders are very strict in regard to repayment terms and persistently follow up with debtors. Payday loans are bad debt that should be avoided at all costs because they compromise your ability to save, affect your credit rating negatively, and sometimes, you lack peace of mind from the constant nagging by the creditors should you delay payment by just a day or two.

Auto loans

An auto loan is used to buy a motor vehicle, structured in installments. Before the loan is released, the financier does a valuation for the automobile and uses it as collateral for the loan.

An auto loan is considered bad debt because a car depreciates quickly. A loan with collateral as a depreciating asset is not only risky but also not worthy. Auto loans have a very high interest rate of about 6% or higher, which means a lot of your monthly income could be spent on repaying the loan. Yet Americans are keen on taking out auto loans to buy their dream cars. They may not be able to afford it, but since most people want to fit in and portray financial abundance, they prefer to purchase cars they cannot afford as opposed to purchasing cars within their financial restraints. The truth is, with proper personal finance planning, it is possible to own a car without getting into debt.

Most auto loan lending companies will entice you with a long-term loan and minimal monthly payments. What most people fail to realize is that by the time they clear the auto loan, they will have paid more for the car as compared with its current market price. Moreover, by the time you clear an auto loan, the car will have depreciated in value significantly. The long-term duration of the automobile loan payment is a disadvantage to the debtor since it attracts very high interest rates. Auto loans may easily go underwater. This means that the value of the car is lower than the outstanding loan amount. This is financially risky because if the car is written off or stolen before fully repaying the auto loan, the insurance company may not be in a position to clear the outstanding loan amount. Such a situation is referred to as negative equity. You would have to repay the outstanding loan amount but have no asset to show for it. Hence, it is advisable to purchase vehicles that you can afford without getting into debt, or, if you must, take as minimal a loan as possible. However, if you take out an auto loan to purchase a business car, the loan may be classified as good debt because it enables you to build wealth.

Chapter Summary

We live in a debt-prone society, and it takes resilience and lots of discipline to avoid falling into the debt trap.

Debt can be good or bad depending on its intended use. Good debt facilitates wealth creation while bad debt eats into your future income and compromises your ability to build wealth.

Most people get into debt due to poor personal financial planning and management skills.

The desire to satiate current needs and uphold a certain lifestyle drives people to make poor financial choices that include getting into debt that later causes stress and, if not careful, poverty.

CHAPTER TWO: TRANSFORMING YOUR RELATIONSHIP WITH DEBT

We live in a society where people may look at you with judgment after realizing you are in debt. Ironically, three out of every five people are in debt. Out of the three, two are drowning in bad debt. Millions of people are stuck in debt and have no way out. They are afraid of disclosing their challenges because of the stigma around debt. Most people will avoid talking about it because they acknowledge that they got into their current situation as a result of poor financial planning; a factor deemed embarrassing. Some of the reasons that get people into debt can be avoided, but people still fall into the debt trap.

PEOPLE FALL INTO DEBT DUE TO PSYCHOLOGICAL AND EMOTIONAL REASONS

There are people who have low self-esteem and are unable to stand against any kind of pressure that comes their way. They seek social status or to belong to a certain clique in an attempt to belong. They tend to overspend in a bid to keep up with the Joneses. By doing so, they get into debt because their income cannot sustain their extravagant lifestyle.

Some people dive into debts in pursuit of happiness. Society has made us believe that we can only be happy if we have money and material possessions like luxury cars and big houses. Many people even believe that you can only be in a happy romantic relationship if you have money. Men especially have been oriented to believe that they can only date the girl they admire if they have money to spend on expensive dinner dates, gifts, or a flashy car. These narratives can land people in debt quickly.

According to the World Health Organization (WHO) report in 2020, one in every four people in the world suffers from mental illness. Occasionally, symptoms of mental illness can cause people to indulge in irresponsible spending. Research reveals that constant worry about debt can trigger stress, which in turn compromises a person's resilience against developing mental illness. Furthermore, mental health issues reduce self-control and affect financial judgment resulting in overspending. Conversely, behavioral patterns that trigger overspending can drive you into debt. (Bill, 2019)

We live in a world that loves partying and competition. In an era where the average person has at least three social media apps on their phone, the influence and competition gathered is immense. People don't want to miss out on the latest events or parties, the newest fashions, or a fancy holiday destination. They all have an imaginary audience that they want to make a statement to. It is unfortunate how people choose to be in debt just to fit in or portray a certain social status.

It's fair to say that a good number of people feel empty inside. This could be anything from lack of purpose to brokenness, their upbringing, or even mental illness, as aforementioned. This emptiness speaks so loudly that you opt to do things that will make you feel special or important, like buying lavish gifts or going on expensive vacations.

This is attributed to the belief that most Americans value instant gratification. There are things we do not need but go ahead and buy because our emotions are directed towards the specific item. The loans people take out to satisfy instant gratification are avoidable if they learn to prioritize needs and live within their means. For example, a good number of Americans incur credit card debt to purchase the latest gadgets, designer outfits, or dine out. These are wants that can be foregone if you do not have the cash to pay for them.

We also tend to define wealth from a standpoint of material possession. However, true and real success is being free from debt. Unfortunately, most people incur debt to purchase goods that depreciate in value and do not generate additional income. The desire to acquire certain social status drives people to make irrational financial decisions that eat into their future income and denies them the ability to invest in wealth creation.

Personally, I got into debt because I wanted to fit in. I was desperate for approval and that led me to overspend as I strived to provide the best I could for my family as well as maintain the new personal lifestyle I had adopted. I was living beyond my means and topped up with loans. This became a vicious cycle because I always had a loan to pay every month. Unfortunately, most people get stuck in debt because they are desperate to maintain a certain social status.

A lot of debt is unnecessary since they are acquired in an effort to live a luxurious lifestyle that cannot be maintained by your salary. We all want a little luxury in our lives, but if that is at the expense of your financial health, then I must say it is not worth it. Live within your means, or better yet, live below your means. If you must fund a fancy lifestyle, then step up and work twice as hard to facilitate it. The importance of a car is to get you to work and that does not require a Lamborghini, a cheaper car will get the job done.

In as much as borrowing money without a plan sounds chaotic, we can all agree that nothing destabilizes your mind like an empty pocket.

EMOTIONAL EFFECTS OF DEBT

Now we are in debt. What happens next? At this point, different emotions are triggered and people often experience depression or anxiety.

According to research conducted by CreditCards.com, around 39% of Americans carry a credit card balance month-to-month, and the average person has around $15,950 in credit card debt. The truth is that whether your debt is "good" or "bad", it will still bother you and can cause serious emotional issues. The average college student graduates with student loans of about $40,000. Students who pursued graduate or higher degrees or switched majors carry even more student loan debt. The Federal Reserve Board Survey released a statement that said at least one in every five borrowers owes $50,000 in student loans, while about 6% of them owe more than $100,000. This means that a good number of American graduates are in debt. Additionally, almost every household has some form of debt from personal loans, mortgages, or auto loans.

Although everybody is affected by debt, the effects manifest differently for different people. Some people feel threatened by and stress out over small loans, while others act like they don't care and continue to take on more debt. Debt is a slippery slope and can cause many types of adverse emotional reactions.

Depression and Anxiety

Dr. John Gathergood of the University of Nottingham conducted a study on the existing relationship between unsettled debts, depression, and anxiety. According to the study, people who were unable to settle their debts and loans have double the chance of experiencing mental health problems; typically depression and anxiety. Anxiety results from constantly worrying about how you will get money, having deep feelings of being overwhelmed with no solutions, and feelings of giving up. Gathergood's study also stated that around 29% of people with high debt experience severe anxiety.

Another study was carried out by social scientists and medics on how physical and mental health is affected by debts. This study (just like Dr. Gathergood's), found that people with high debt are vulnerable to higher rates of stress and depression. The Royal College of psychiatrists gathered and studied the findings of more than fifty research papers on the subject. All the research had a common theme, that people with tendencies of high debt expressed symptoms of depression.

Resentment

Financial strain can even put people in a state of resentment as a coping mechanism, especially in relationships, partnerships, families, and marriages. According to Sonya Britt, an Assistant Professor of Family Studies at Kansas State University, financial disagreements are among the leading causes of divorce. The Royal College of psychiatrists also concluded that large amounts of debt immensely affect the household's psychological well-being. This resentment might also include rejecting your employer for paying you a lesser amount of money, or not promoting you, leading you to borrow more to sustain your livelihood. You might also feel resentment toward your family or friends. Your family may be dependent on you, affecting your financial status, and perhaps your friends are in a better financial position. You might find yourself blaming people or situations for your current financial position. For example, blaming your lecturers or parents for not educating you on the implication of student loans. Worst of all, you might resent yourself for not making wise financial decisions. Self-resentment comes with tones of regret.

Denial

As mentioned earlier, people have different ways of dealing with debt. Some decide to ignore their thoughts about the amount they owe. But, being in denial of your debt (even after constant reminders) is not uncommon. The most unfortunate thing about ignoring debts is that no matter how good you are at ignoring it, you will only be relieved for a very short period. The relief might even cause you to accumulate more debts. Eventually, you will wind up with a very large burden of debt to settle.

You know you are in denial of your debt when you intentionally ignore opening bills and bank statements, accumulating bills and late notices in a drawer, and pretending to forget about them. When you fail to pick up phone calls from new or unrecognized numbers that you presume they belong to creditors, or when you make an intentional decision not to do anything about debts, that is denial.

Living in denial is one of the worst things you could do, because you will do nothing to pay down what you owe, and will probably continue spending even more. Once you have a loan it accrues interest daily, monthly, or annually, depending on the agreement you have with your financier, and failing to repay might incur penalties and interest, which will be part of the money that you owe moving forward.

Stress

You will get stressed over debts even if you ignore the fact that you owe people or financial institutions money. You keep wondering if you will ever manage to get out of debt and what would be the best strategy to do it. The higher the debt, the more stressful it gets. Racing thoughts about debt may also affect your productivity at work. You may be motivated to give your job all you got because you depend on it to settle bills and pay down debt. However, most people become less productive because they are unable to concentrate at work. Moreover, anytime you have a need that must be solved with money, you are under more pressure and stress.

According to a study conducted by the American Psychological Association in 2019, at least 64% of graduate students admitted that being in debt interrupted their normal functioning. People with debt are more likely to suffer poor physical health, according to a study by the Associated Press. Poor physical health is triggered by stress, anxiety, and depression. Studies have shown that the higher your debt is, the more likely you are to suffer depression and stress. Apart from disrupting your daily productivity, debt-induced stress triggers negative attitudes, even towards meaningful and helpful situations. According to Ryan Howell, an Associate Professor of Psychology at San Francisco State University, stress can prevent you from enjoying all the privileges and happiness that is found in spending money.

Anger and Frustration

Anger and frustration are powerful, instinctive, and natural emotions. Being angry and frustrated can be attributed to being threatened or attacked mentally, verbally, or physically. When you have a huge debt burden, it is not uncommon to feel angry and frustrated about the situation, especially if your current income is not sufficient to cover the debt. Worse still, being in debt can take a toll on your emotional well-being. Being angry and frustrated is one way of coping with the debt situation. In most cases, people get frustrated because they barely have enough assets to show for the huge amount of debt they have incurred. The anger and frustration get intense when you realize the number of financial sacrifices you must make to get out of debt. You may even feel guilty at how you got into debt initially, especially if you took out debt for instant gratification. But, once you get over the denial, fear, anger, and frustration of being in debt, you will be able to acknowledge the situation and work to pay down the debts gradually, and eventually, work towards staying out of debt. It is important to accept your situation and focus on moving forward by making better financial decisions in a bid to avoid falling back into the debt trap.

Regret

I bet that most of us have found ourselves regretting some decisions we made that cost us more than we were ready to pay for. That's the same thing with debt, you will borrow today and be excited about acquiring the car of your dreams, but when debt accumulates, you begin to regret your decisions. When thoughts of the money we owe cross our mind, we are likely to wish we never took out a loan, that we never made certain purchases, or maybe that we should have saved enough money for the days when we are drowning in debt. Students who took out loans to pay for their college degrees wish they searched for scholarships or applied for financial aid. Some students never took the time to understand the loans they were being granted when they began college. Perhaps they would have borrowed less or even worked out a plan on how to graduate debt-free.

Dread

Being in debt can bring about feelings of dread. For example, an activity like shopping for insurance frustrates you to the point that you don't want to do it. Then you get into more trouble financially since credit scores and insurance go hand in hand. You decide to ignore the issue and end up paying more, sometimes triple, the initial amount. You may know that you are spending too much on an apartment, but you are not able to move out because you feel the process is too long. Yet you could find a cheaper, nicer apartment and save some money. That could go a long way in paying off debt. This attitude toward debt will surely destroy your finances even more. It takes you away from reason and puts you in a place where everything seems impossible. Meanwhile, you are still accumulating more debt.

Shame and Embarrassment

We might try to run from it, but our society defines success by being directly proportional to the material possessions you own. It's no shock that when you are in debt you will feel ashamed or embarrassed about it. The embarrassment may be because you do not make a lot of money or you lack financial management skills. Thus, you fell into the trap of debt. That's why you are not able to live up to the standards you desire. The American Psychological Association says that most graduate students feel ashamed of the piling educational loans they have because they do not yet have well-paying jobs.

It is fair to categorize debt as taboo since it is one of those topics that nobody wants to talk about. We find it so hard to sit down with our families and friends to tell them how we are in debt. In 2019 CreditCard.com conducted a survey and around 85% of the respondents were not comfortable disclosing their credit card debt. It is about time we dropped this attitude and started opening up about our finances. Remaining silent will lead us to more debt. You will continue spending because you will not be able to say no to family and friends about things you cannot afford since you want to keep proving you have money when you don't.

Fear

Owing someone money that you are unable to pay is almost similar to slavery. This is because it keeps you within the fear of the unknown. You keep worrying about how your financier can come to collect the debt, how you can be evicted from your home, go bankrupt, or get your utilities disconnected. You live in fear of unforeseen catastrophe, like losing your job or your car breaking down, because that will only hurt your finances more. You fear what is going to happen next now that you have accumulated debt. There is also the fear of losing relationships because the people you owe money to may be close friends or family, or because you have cut them off as a coping mechanism. The University of Wisconsin Madison carried out research that concludes that most young adults fear marriage or are divorced due to a high level of debt.

Relief, Freedom, and Accomplishment

After all is said and done, you must accept your financial situation and deal with it without feeling guilty, stressed, or frustrated. Once you have fully settled your debt, positive emotions tag along. Trent Hamm, The Simple Dollar founder, once said that debt freedom is not just freedom from debt. Its freedom from worry. Settling your debts also translates to an improvement in your mental and physical health.

We all want to enjoy the freedom of being debt-free, of being at peace with ourselves, and of maintaining good relationships. For you to attain this there are several things you need to put in your mind.

Think about what is triggering your spending and deal with it, either by avoiding it or by seeking alternative measures to satisfy it. If it is the desire to live a good life, then work hard, and live it, but do not take out loans to fund what you cannot afford. We have been told to live within our means more than enough times, but that is easier said than done. You will need to cultivate discipline and adhere to a budget. If it is the need for approval, change your mindset so that you are content with whom you are and what you have. You can choose to cut off certain friends or family who pressure you to indulge in activities that ruin your financial status. Seek help or find ways of coping with mental illness, stress, and boredom instead of allowing yourself to spend too much trying to tame it with activities like shopping or partying.

You should not feel ashamed of debt, just willing to conquer it. It's okay that you brought yourself into the situation, but it will require you to get out of it. Accept that you spent your money in the wrong way. Admit to yourself that you are a poor financial manager and begin to research smart money moves that you can implement for better financial standing. Ignoring the fact that you owe somebody or institution money does not negate that fact you are in debt and you must pay it off. The permanent solution to debt is facing it head-on and dealing with it.

Talk about your debt situation with people you trust to ease the emotional burden. Part of the depression you get into while in debt can be a result of not speaking out and getting ideas of how to negate the problem. The first stage of overcoming this is admitting that you are in debt and you are not ashamed of it because you are going to get out of it. After you have forgiven yourself for the bad financial decisions, then go ahead and talk to somebody about what you are going through. The person might not help you pay your debts but speaking up will relieve you of the emotional burden. The person you open up to will keep you accountable, remind you to make better choices in the future, and might even offer a solution; maybe give you an idea of a second source of income that could help you solve your financial crisis.

Do not ignore your debt. It might feel like a safe idea to ignore it, but it is not a solution. It's time to take the bull by the horns. Make peace with the situation and accept it as it is. Pay off what you can and save yourself from accumulating more.

You could be in debt to the point where you feel like it is impossible to pay it off. The truth is you can settle those debts, and it's not impossible to do so. You just need to be intentional about it and take the first step of repaying. Taking simple repayment steps, even if you are paying very little money, is better than the comfort of watching your interest accumulate and losing your sanity. Paying off your loans will see you gain control over your finances again. After you are done paying off your debts, make wise decisions with your money, and save for the future. Do not relapse to old spending habits, but instead work to make better ones.

Chapter Summary

People fall into the debt trap due to poor personal finance management skills and above all, the desire for instant gratification.

The emotional side effects of debt include; fear, stress, frustration, shame, anger, resentment, and depression.

These side effects can be avoided by sharing your debt problems with a person you trust, accepting the situation, and working to pay off the debt.

CHAPTER THREE: TAKING STOCK OF YOUR CURRENT SITUATION

In the previous chapter, we talked about the stage of acceptance. Acknowledging your debt is the first step towards redeeming your financial situation. In this chapter, we will learn what to do next. Only a fool comes to terms with their weaknesses and does nothing about it. There are many strategies and small changes you can make to settle your debts. The first question you may ask yourself is, "Now that I have come to terms with my financial situation, what do I do next? Will I be able to get out of this?" And my answer to you is YES! It may not be easy; it takes discipline and intentional decisions. Let's look at ten ways to help you get out of debt.

STEPS TO IMPROVE YOUR FINANCIAL SITUATION

1. Assess your current finances

The starting point of ending debt is knowing where you currently stand financially. This overview will give you a chance to come up with a plan that will help you get to your desired financial state. One of the best ways of determining your current financial state is by calculating your net worth; the value of your assets vis-a-vis your liabilities. Using a spreadsheet, record all of your assets and liabilities. Subtract your total liabilities from your total assets to find your net worth. The result you get should help you make better financial decisions and set goals that propel you towards a debt-free and financially stable life. This is because you are able to determine the amount of assets you own and the financial liabilities that may be hindering you from acquiring your desired net worth. In light of this, you can reduce liabilities and redirect the extra money towards investing in assets and ultimately increase your net worth.

2. Set financial goals

After assessing your current financial state, the next step is setting your future financial goals. Your goals should be realistic so that they feel attainable, but aggressive enough to get you out of your comfort zone. For instance, if you have to increase your income in order to achieve your saving target or pay off debt faster, you can consider a part-time job. Most Americans have liabilities that exceed their assets so if you fall into this category, you are not alone (Miriam, 2020).

A good net worth is one whose financial and non-financial assets exceed liabilities despite their amount but there is no base value of what a good net worth should be. It all depends on personal finance goals. However, it varies based on age whereby you are expected to have a higher net worth at retirement as compared to when young or fresh out of college. It takes time, focus, and dedication to build a good net worth. Therefore, if you find out that your net worth is below what you want it to be, determine your goals, write them down, and work on meeting them. Writing your goals down will remind you of your desired financial future, and will also serve as a reminder of how hard you need to work to attain them. You could come up with ways of increasing savings such as starting a business or getting a promotion or salary increase.

3. **Create a budget**

As you were analyzing your financial situation in the previous steps, you might have already realized some of the reasons you are not progressing financially, or why you have too much bad debt. However, in order for you to successfully plan your financial future, you will need to come up with a monthly budget and see where, and how much, you are spending. Begin by subtracting your total monthly expenses from your monthly income. If the balance is zero or negative, you must make some decisions to cut costs. Some of the easiest places to cut costs are food and entertainment. You can reduce how much you spend on entertainment or choose to cook food at home instead of dining out.

If the amount you get after subtracting expenses from your income is positive, come up with a budget on how you will be spending money monthly. You can use the envelope way of budgeting. You will put a different amount of money into different envelopes and label them with what the money is supposed to do. Make sure you stick to your budget by appropriately allocating every dollar of your income. This step might lead you to adjust your lifestyle a bit; which could be uncomfortable, but it will be worth it when you achieve your personal financial goals.

TACKLE YOUR DEBT

Your financial situation will only get better if you stick to your budget and pay off your debt. Regardless of how much you owe, or how impossible it may appear, you must continue to pay it off anyway. Every payment helps. Alternatively, the longer you take to repay, the more you will ultimately pay because of interest accumulation.

You need to come up with a plan. List all your debt in order from highest to lowest, the interest rates, minimum payments, and due dates. Determine which debts are growing fastest due to their interest rates. Once you have made this list, you will know which debt to pay down first. Each month, make all your payments, then direct any extra money to that particular debt you want to get rid of first. Repay the first and then keep moving down your list until you fully settle all of them.

If you feel as if your debts are not manageable, a good strategy to gain momentum is to pick the lowest and repay it. Once you see progress after clearing an entire debt, you will be motivated to continue. Do not give up on repayment, even if you feel like you are not making progress. Instead motivate yourself with the end game in mind: financial freedom. If you have any debts that are in collection, begin by repaying them first and bringing them to current so that you can reduce the negative impact on your credit. This will keep you from receiving those annoying calls from your creditors. As you pay off your debt, you absolutely must refrain from using credit cards or acquiring more debt.

Control your expenditures

The next steps will put your discipline to the test, but they will be instrumental in helping you stick to your budget and stave off the behaviors that initially got you into debt. Once you get a handle on your expenditures, you might discover you have a bit of money left over that you could use to pay down your debt faster. Controlling your expenses begins by identifying any hidden costs that may not be included in your budget.

If you have a family, consider cooking at home rather than ordering food from a restaurant. This will save you a good amount of money and your family will enjoy healthy, home-cooked meals. Sounds like a win-win, right? Consider simply leaving your credit card at home to avoid the temptation to spend. Evaluate your bills again and do away with any service you are not using; like gym memberships, streaming services, or monthly subscriptions. These savings can be put toward extra payments or building savings for the future.

Address your income

You may try to implement all these suggestions, but still realize your finances are poor. You may realize you have cash flow issues and live paycheck to paycheck. This could be a result of your extravagance, perhaps you do not pay attention to the price of things. You should always compare prices before you buy anything. If the quality is the same, then always opt for the less expensive option. The strain to pay bills could also be the reason as to why you got into debt.

If your income issue is temporary, you could try to look for an alternative source of income or a second job. However, if the problem is persistent, you might decide to make more intense decisions to help your budget, such as moving to an area where the cost of living is low or go back to school to get qualifications for a promotion and higher income.

Consider an emergency fund

Life is unpredictable and at any time you could be faced with unexpected issues that may cause financial strain, such as a sick family member, a car accident, or the death of a family member. For such issues, ensure you have good health, home, car, and life insurance coverage. When we are in financial constraints, insurance seems like a luxury, but when one of these calamities strike, they might affect your finances in a way that will take you a very long period of time to recover. Insurance helps cover you when faced by unexpected situations and so you can sort them without breaking the bank.

In your budget, remember to allocate a few funds for the emergency kitty. This will help you grow it without feeling burdened. You should only withdraw from your emergency fund in case of an emergency. A good rule of thumb is to have enough savings to cover your expenses for three to six months. In the event you need it, for example, if you lost your job or were in an accident, it will cover you for the period of time you are not able to work.

Build a habit of saving

If I told you saving is easy, I would be lying. Saving requires discipline; a habit you build over time. It can be hard to save instead of spend, but if you have to attain financial freedom, then saving is one of those things you will have to embrace. Create a way of maximizing your savings through things like buying in bulk, comparing prices and settling for cheaper options, buying second-hand items, buying goods that are on sale, or using coupons. This will ensure you stretch your budget further and find some money to put towards savings.

One way of cultivating financial discipline is by having a sinking fund. A sinking fund functions like an emergency fund except it is supposed to support planned investments. If you need to save for something, like a home, for example, determine how much you need and the timeline you want to work with. That will guide how much you will need to save and how long it will take to save it. Make sure you stick with your goals no matter how strenuous feels.

Create a solid financial plan

By creating a solid financial plan, you create a financially secure future. As much as you are paying your loans and saving for upcoming expenses, do not forget your long-term financial goals. Develop a plan that will help you grow your wealth. Some of these strategies are having a retirement plan and making long-term investments that will continue to earn you money when you will not have the strength to go to your 9-5 job.

Financial experts say that you should first pay off your debt before you embark on making investments. Make sure you talk to an expert about your goals and income. This will help you get the best advice and strategies.

Don't entertain discouragement

Sometimes when we are overwhelmed by situations, we think about giving up. Finances are no different. The most important thing is to stay motivated by the fact that the future is getting better even though you are cutting some expenses today. Getting out of debt will be worth it. Keep yourself accountable by sharing your goals with friends and family that you trust. Try not to be too hard on yourself. Set small and realistic goals. Reward yourself every time you hit a major milestone. Simply remain committed and patient with yourself, and eventually, your financial situation will improve.

Sell off Investments

Does selling off investments to pay debts sound like a good idea? This is dependent on your school of thought. However, the question you should be asking yourself instead is, "Is remaining in debt a good idea?" The longer you remain in debt the more money you will spend paying off interests. Holding on to debt negatively affects your credit score, which may hinder you from securing a future loan or making it more expensive the next time you need to borrow money. If you are overwhelmed by debt and you do not have any other means of repaying it, then selling off some of your investments is a reasonable strategy.

If you decide to sell some of your investments to repay your debt, you will need to do some research. Make a comparison of the amount of interest your debt accumulates versus the interest you make from your investments. If the interest earned by investments is lower, then it's wise to liquidate that asset and use the proceeds to pay off debt. If you have several assets or investments, consider the one that has the lowest return and sell it. This will give you a leg up financially because you will have paid off some debt, but still kept one or some of the investments that provide healthy returns.

When selling investments, do not be so desperate to get rid of them that you're willing to take a loss. Sometimes people think selling an investment at a loss is beneficial because it lowers your tax charges, but you should be less interested in tax relief than in making a profit. You should opt to hold on a little longer to make sure you can sell it at a good profit.

There are debts that can be settled via other means, like low-interest debt, mortgage, and hospital bills. Only "bad debt" like credit cards or payday loans should call for such decisions. Because the interest rates are so high and you might end up paying triple the amount you originally owed. Also, consider the type of investment you are selling. Long-term investments attract more tax than short-term.

Debt cycle

As aforementioned, debt can be good or bad; it's good when used to build your net worth but eventually, it must be paid off. If for some reason you are unable to pay off debt, you are bound to fall in a debt cycle that is hard to get out of. Good debt, such as mortgages and student loans, are almost inevitable. This is because most people cannot afford it while only relying on their income. If you add auto loans and credit cards to the mix, then you might find yourself enslaved to debt. Entertaining the idea of taking payday loans or other high-interest loans will pull you into a debt cycle quickly. However, you need to pay off your debt so you don't rack up more interest. Failing to be intentional about paying your debts can lead you to a debt cycle that will make it impossible for you to be financially independent. It could also affect your monthly income during repayment.

A debt cycle is continuous borrowing without repaying the first loan, thus increasing the applicable interest costs and ultimately, default penalties due to financial strains. Most debts are brought about by spending more than you earn. Some people take out loans to pay off existing loans or just to keep up with the required minimum payments. However, sometimes it makes sense to borrow a new loan that will assist you in paying off the existing loan. Debt consolidation helps you reduce the amount of interest to be paid if you took longer to pay the loan. Loans are a problem when using them to fund your day-to-day activities rather than investing in your future.

HOW TO AVOID THE DEBT CYCLE

Seek alternative sources of income to avoid the debt cycle. Set a budget and realistic expenses that will help you avoid borrowing money to cover your bills. Avoiding indulging in additional debt. Create a solid financial plan, maintain discipline, and focus on attaining financial freedom. Unless you are able to pay your credit card bills on a monthly basis, avoid them totally.

When borrowing money, keep in mind that lenders do not have you in mind. This is business, and they are after profit. Never borrow the maximum amount, instead borrow only what you need. Make sure you have a plan in mind before going to mortgage lenders or auto dealers. They have ways of convincing you to take the maximum monthly payment. Conduct your due diligence and have comparisons of different products as well as loan packages. Always go for the cheaper option if the quality is not compromised. Better to have a less expensive car than get stuck in debt with a luxury one.

Make it a habit to buy only what you need. Just because you can afford something does not mean you should spend money on it. Stick to your monthly budget unless something is really necessary or an emergency. You should live well within your means, but it would be even better to live below your means. This will not only help you to avoid debts but it will also help you save for the future and make major investments. Following these suggestions and avoiding the debt cycle will bring you financial independence.

If you are in a position where you can afford to pay off your debt, but you allow yourself to be stuck in a cycle of debt, it causes more harm to your finances.

Diagnosing your financial situation

Many people do not know where they stand financially, because they are scared to confront their financial situations. Everyone wants more money and less stress. But stress is inevitable if you want to address your debt issues and ultimately, your financial standing. The first step is diagnosing where you are. At this stage, you should make peace with whatever findings you come up with. If you have poor spending habits, this is the point where you forgive yourself and decide to start all over again. You must consider how much money you have and how much you spend.

We have two types of expenses; fixed and variable. Fixed expenses are recurring expenses that do not change in value month after month, like house rent, mortgage payments, and utility bills. Variable expenses change each month, like groceries or dining out. Your optimum goal should be spending less and saving more.

Savings to pay off debt

Is it okay to use savings to pay off debt? It is not enticing to break into your savings to pay debt. It is discouraging because you may feel like you have nothing to show after years of hard work. However, it could save you from an unhealthy financial state in the long run. Using your savings to pay off debt is definitely a good alternative.

It's likely that your savings are earning less interest than the amount your debt is accumulating in terms of interest. Using your savings to pay off debt will help you pay less interest, which we should use in your payment period and you can embark on saving again. Clearing your debt as soon as possible is better than having savings in the bank.

Before you consider using your savings to pay off debts, decide if it's cost-effective to do so. For example, if you have a 0% balance transfer card all your money is outstanding on an interest-free overdraft, then it's not necessary to use your savings to pay it since it's not accumulating any interest. Instead, you should use savings to repay debts that are accumulating interest. Considering such factors will help you keep some of your savings while also taming financial distress.

> Is it appropriate for you to spend all your savings and be left with nothing?

The answer to this question varies from person to person depending on your financial situation. If you know of a situation that you will need money for in the near future, then you can consider keeping some savings for it. If you can pay your debt using alternative means, without necessarily using your savings, that could turn out to be a good idea.

Emergency fund

How much you save in your emergency fund is dependent on a number of things; your income, your expenditures, the number of people depending on you, and your monthly costs. Ideally, you should have enough money to last at least six months. Saving up such a large amount of money might seem impossible. But if you choose to save little by little until you get to the targeted goal, it will not be overwhelming. Set realistic goals for your savings. Take into consideration your income, expenditures, and monthly payments before settling for the total amount of money you can contribute to your emergency fund. The trick is to always contribute to your emergency fund, no matter how small, but do not forego doing so.

When setting aside an emergency fund, make sure you keep the money in an interest-earning venture such as money markets or a bank account that will earn interest. Make sure the process of getting your money is seamless. Since this money is supposed to be for emergencies, you don't want to struggle with the withdrawal process when you need the cash. Avoid accounts that will charge you penalties or taxes. The disadvantage of putting emergency savings in mutual funds or stock markets is that they may lose value, and it will be harder for you to withdraw your money when the time rises. That's why you should use a savings account that will not charge you in case of early withdrawals.

Ensure the money you've saved in the emergency fund is only used in case of an emergency. Once you've used funds from this account make sure you record how much and replenish it after you've settled the emergency. These savings go a long way in supporting you during an unexpected time so do not give up on it once you've used the money; make sure you rebuild it.

Subscriptions

Nowadays, most companies try to entice individuals with long-term subscriptions. The subscriptions could be monthly, quarterly, or even annually. It has been made as easy as possible for you to sign up via your phone or through various applications. Due to the ease of the process, most people find themselves having a handful of subscriptions that could translate to hundreds of dollars. Unfortunately, most people end up not even using some of these subscriptions. That's a lot of money to go to waste. This should be a wake-up call for everyone to check on their subscriptions. All that money could go a long way in building financial freedom through savings or investments.

A good example is cable TV. Many people are opting to "cut the cord" to save money. This is because you can choose the shows you want on subscription and connect to the free antenna to broadcast the local channels.

Ideally, the purpose of subscription services is entertainment. If used well, they can be great, but if you are not keen, you might end up wasting a lot of money and living beyond your budget. Subscriptions should be part of your monthly plan. Stick to what you planned for and do not sign up for additional subscriptions. Pay close attention to how much you are spending and periodically check in to make sure you are getting value for your money. Only paying for what you are using will keep you from spending money on something you really do not need.

Take away note

Before opting to use cash for debt settlement, analyze your risk tolerance. Risk tolerance is your ability to stand losses that may occur in your investment choices. You cannot predict the exact losses that will occur, but you can assess the situation and come up with a rough idea.

The factors that will influence the dominant risk include your age, income, amount of time to retirement, expenditures, and your individual tax situation. For example, it is easier for young people to make riskier types of investment. This is because they have more time left to make mistakes. They are also at a good age for working, which means if they incurred a loss, they can more easily bounce back since they still have a salary.

Chapter Summary

The first step towards getting out of debt is determining your current financial standing to determine the amount you can set aside for debt repayment.

Prioritize debt payment over investment.

Every financial decision you make should be geared towards improving your financial situation.

CHAPTER FOUR: TACKLING YOUR DEBT

ENGAGING THE CREDITORS

Sometimes things like job loss, salary reductions, or medical emergencies strike and leave you in a bad financial position that you never anticipated. In such times, you may not be in a position to make your monthly payments. In many cases, people stop making monthly payments when their income is compromised, however, it is always advisable to reach out to your bank or credit card company to explain your current financial situation and possibly strike a new, more affordable payment plan.

Why engage creditors?

Though the process of reporting information every other month to credit reporting agencies is voluntary, that information will affect your credit report. As such, failure to honor your loan repayment as agreed upon will negatively impact your credit report. However, creditors always have some discretion about how negative the information they submit to the credit reporting agencies is; they may file a less damaging report based on your level of cooperation even when you have defaulted on payment for months. Therefore, if a rocky situation arises, taking a proactive role to engage with your creditor and explain your current financial situation can get them to show mercy while filing your monthly report.

Notifying creditors about your current financial strain may not be reason enough for them not to file a negative report. You may need to negotiate with them. A good, positive credit report is important if you intend to take out loans in the future. Moreover, a good credit score grants you access to better credit facilities, terms, and interest rates.

Negotiating your financial obligations opens up options for you. For instance, you may get reduced monthly payments, penalties or fees waived, your interest rate lowered, or better still, restructure your loan based on your current financial position. Depending on how well you negotiate, your ability to pay a lump sum amount, and your financial situation, you could get up to a 50 percent loan waiver.

TIPS ON HOW TO NEGOTIATE WITH CREDITORS

As you approach your lender for negotiations, keep in mind that their job is to recover the money owed to them. This is business, after all. It is your responsibility to protect your interests while upholding your financial and legal responsibilities. Negotiating may be harder if you are dealing with a collection agency representative. Their goal is to collect the due payments; their best interests lie with the company they represent and not necessarily with you. No matter how long you have defaulted on loan repayment or how much you owe your creditor, never avoid them. Avoiding or ignoring your creditor only worsens your situation.

Initial contact

It is important that you know and understand your rights before setting up a meeting with your creditor. This is because, despite the fact that debt collection agencies are governed by the Fair Debt Collection Practices Act and other state-specific statutes, they are notorious in violating the laws (David, 2019). But, if you understand your rights as a debtor before approaching them, you will be negotiating from a strong and informed position. Information is power!

In most cases, when a debtor defaults on numerous monthly payments, the creditors and debt collection agencies call every day to demand payments. If you find yourself in such a position, the best way to initiate a negotiation is by informing the caller that you are willing to settle the loan. Go ahead and request to speak with the right person with the aim of discussing a debt settlement plan. If the creditor does not call you, it is your responsibility to initiate contact by calling them to book an appointment.

During your meeting with the creditor, be confident and decisive. Expect respect, but be respectful. Feel free to ask for clarification if you do not understand the terms or what the expectations are. Above all, do not agree to anything unless it is put down in writing.

Negotiation strategy

The general credit negotiation strategy is suggesting paying as little as possible on the outstanding loan balance. However, this must be in line with what the creditor is ready to accept. In most cases, they will ask for a lump sum payment over regular monthly payments. Therefore, the best strategy is to offer the creditors a lump sum payment but at a reduced amount. For instance, if your credit card loan balance is $10,000 you can offer to pay a lump sum amount of $5,000 within a certain period of time. You must be sure that you will be in a position to honor the agreed-upon lump sum payment and as per the terms.

Before engaging the creditors, determine what you will be negotiating for. This could include things like a lower interest rate; waiver of accrued interests; waiver of applicable legal fees, late payment fees, and penalties; restructuring or extension of the loan, which allows you to skip some months without incurring penalties; a convenient and affordable payment plan that allows you to pay for the loan balance; lower balance settlement; and of course, favorable reporting to the credit report agencies and removal of any negative credit information that may have been filed.

Always start by giving the creditors a low payment offer. Never make an offer based on the highest amount you are able to pay, whether as a regular or a lump sum payment. This is because the creditors will always counter your offer by increasing your suggested amount. Starting low means that the creditors will suggest an amount that is closer to the range you are able to settle without as much strain.

During the negotiation, ensure that you maintain a positive attitude and tone. People are always more willing to reason and work with people who are professional, respectful, and positive. Your goal is to get a debt settlement agreement that works for you.

Once you have reached an agreement, it is important to have the settlement agreement in writing. This protects you from future harassment by the creditor. A settlement agreement should be mandatory in case you had been sued by the creditor for failing to honor your loan payment. Though it incurs extra attorney expenses, it is in your best interest to have the settlement agreement in writing.

Note that debt settlement helps you avoid filing for

bankruptcy. You will have to convince all your creditors to offer an amicable debt settlement yet some might not be willing since it means that they lose part of their profit from your loan. Additionally, the creditors will report the debt settlement to the credit reporting agencies and this will lower your credit rating. In some cases, a debt settlement is considered a taxable gain. Therefore, you should consult an accountant to ensure that you honor your taxes as well.

Make and Follow a Budget

Financial surveys reveal that most American households struggle with debt and do not have enough savings to cover emergencies of $1,000. It's clear to see the value of developing and adhering to budgets. However, you may be skeptical about budgeting because you'd have to change your spending habits and sometimes that means cutting down on activities you deem fun, like partying, vacations, eating in restaurants, or shopping. A budget defines how much you make and how you spend your income, so it is a very important personal finance tool that shapes your financial future for the better when well utilized.

Regardless of age or economic standing, everyone benefits from creating and adhering to a budget. A budget gives you a sense of control over your income and future financial well being. A well-developed budget sets the financial foundation for the future.

Creating a budget

There are different ways of creating and monitoring your budget. The different techniques vary based on age and current financial standing. However, there are basic steps that should be followed when creating a reasonable and workable budget that ensure that you organize your finances appropriately, and above all, get out of debt. The steps include:

1. Goal setting

There are two main types of financial goals; short-term and long-term. Short-term goals focus on things that require you to spend money immediately while long-term goals are focused on saving and spending money in the future. Short-term and long-term financial goals complement each other because your short-term spending habits determine your ability to save and spend money in the future.

Immediate financial goals focus on meeting current financial needs which may be obligatory or secondary. Obligatory goals include buying household supplies, food, rent, mortgage payments, car payments, utilities, or childcare. Secondary goals are things that we like but we can live without such as vacations, dining out, non-essential clothing, and subscriptions. On the other hand, long-term financial goals could be things like saving for retirement, making investments, or charitable donations. Budgeting begins with determining necessities and luxuries in a bid to make financial planning easier. Paying down debt is classified as a short-term goal that ensures financial solvency. But, paying off your debts earlier than the due date makes long-term sense because you will have more money to save or spend in the future.

2. Calculate income and expenses

The next step after determining your short-term and long-term financial goals is determining how you will achieve them. To do that, you must evaluate your current income and expenditures. Most individuals and households resonate with monthly budgets because bills are paid monthly. To create your monthly budget, you should start by gathering all your financial statements. In this case, financial statements are all documents that highlight your monthly income and expenses. They include; bank statements, credit card accounts, records of monthly bills, paycheck stubs, and investment accounts among others.

Note, the strength and effectiveness of a budget are determined by how accurate and relevant it is. Therefore, evaluate at least three months of the credit card, debit card, bank, and utility bill statements to ensure that you have a precise picture of your income and expenses. Though income and expenditure patterns vary from one month to another, the best way to know your spending pattern is by gathering a paper trail from the past three months.

When determining your income, take-home income is all that counts, do not factor in additional one time earnings like occasional work tips. Your take-home income includes your after-tax salary, regular bonuses, alimony payments, child support, social security, pension, dividend, or interest earnings. List all your income sources and the amount you get from each one and add them up. The total is the take-home income you should work with to develop a budget. Once you determine your monthly income, the next step is determining your expenses. Expenses fall into three main categories; fixed, variable, and discretionary.

Fixed expenses: these are expenses that remain consistent every month. They mainly cater to needs rather than wants, but the more you spend on fixed expenses the less financially flexible you will be to make adjustments when the need arises. Fixed expenses include rent, mortgage payments, insurance, utility bills, car payments, or loans.

Variable expenses: these are expenses that vary from one month to the next, depending on the household spending habits and lifestyle choices. Variable expenses are typically wants that can be adjusted to reallocate budget for personal finance goals. They include things like gasoline or groceries.

Discretionary expenses: these are optional expenses that cater to services or items that you can do without like entertainment, recreation, or dining out. Discretionary expenses make life fun, more fulfilling, and to some extent easier. However, they should always be the first to be eliminated if your income is not sufficient to cover the basic requirements like housing, groceries, and repayment of debts.

3. Analyze your spending vis-a-vis your income

Now that you have determined your income and expenses, the next step is to analyze them. Add up your monthly expenses and see whether they exceed your income or if you have some excess cash that can be used to pay off debt or build an emergency account. The main goal of creating a budget is to ensure that your expenses do not exceed your income. In case your expenses do exceed your income, it means that you live beyond your means and you end up needing to borrow every other month to pay for expenses. Therefore, you need to make adjustments in a bid to cut down on borrowing and have some excess cash that you can dedicate to paying off debt.

Revisit your variable and discretionary expenses to determine what you can and are willing to do without. Based on your compiled list of expenses, you should be able to tell how much you spend on discretionary expenses. These are things you can live without as you reorganize your finances to get extra money for debt repayment. Although adjusting to less spending on these kinds of expenses may be hard, it is a choice you make to ensure that you have a better and more stable financial future.

If you find that adjusting variable and discretionary expenses does not yield enough to cover debt payments as well as meet your saving goals, consider adjusting your fixed expenses as well. If necessary, opt for a cheaper apartment or home, shop for a less expensive car insurance plan, and if you have a high-maintenance car, research alternatives. To ensure that you do not miss out on fixed payments or incur late payment charges, consider setting up automatic payments with your bank. Alternatively, have a bill calendar to help you keep tabs on due dates. Late payment charges and penalties can throw your budget off track in terms of late fees and penalties. In the end, you save less and derail your long-term financial goals.

BUDGETING APPROACH

Determining your budget and cutting down on expenses is only half the battle. Most people are unable to determine the amount they should set aside for savings as well as debt payments. You should aim to have a reasonable balance based on your available disposable income. Failure to set the right financial goals when you budget will render the endeavor futile. Choosing the right income allocation budgeting approach is crucial to ensure that the budgeting process and sacrifices you make pay off.

Though there are numerous budgeting approaches, the 50-30-20 budget model by Senator Elizabeth Warren works for many because of its simplicity and clarity. It advocates for the division of income into three parts where 50% is allocated to payment of basic expenses like rent, food, and minimum payment on debts, 30% is allocated to variable and discretionary expenses like entertainment, while the remaining 20% is dedicated to building an emergency fund, saving, and potentially additional payment of debts. Your monthly savings should include building an emergency fund that can sustain you for at least six months should your source of income be compromised.

As with other budgeting approaches, this one also comes with exceptions. For instance, low-income earners that are deep in debt may have to dedicate more of their income to debt repayment. On the other hand, affluent households may be in a position to save 20% or more of their income should they opt to forego luxuries like buying expensive cars or booking expensive hotels during vacation. Due to such income variations, it is recommended that you save at least 10% of your monthly income for emergencies. This mainly applies to low-income households that are struggling to pay off debt and cover fixed expenses.

The 10% income allocation to savings may not be much but it is only temporary until you are able to offset debt or get a higher paying job that leaves you with more disposable income. Additionally, it is highly advisable to uphold the minimized spending patterns even after you get out of debt. This ensures that you do not fall back into the debt trap and above all, you save more for long-term goals as well as emergencies that drive people to take out expensive payday loans.

Envelope Style Budgeting

Envelope style budgeting is a systemic and simple model of paying bills and saving money. It works because it ensures that you set aside the amount you need for bills in a manner that coerces you to uphold a personal budget. It is a popular budgeting model that works for a lot of people despite their level of income and can be implemented using personal finance software. It advocates for the division of income into different spending groups like utility bills, groceries, rent, loans, and gas. Once you have budgeted what you will spend on every category, you place the actual cash amount in an envelope and label it accordingly. Throughout the month, you are only allowed to spend what is in each envelope for its particular category of expense. This limits overspending since you can only spend what is available in the envelopes. Once an envelope is empty, you stop spending on that particular category until the following month.

The envelope style budget advocates for use of cash and debit cards as opposed to credit cards. Debit cards are ideal when budgeting using financial software and cash is ideal if you are following the envelope system as discussed above. If you need to buy something or pay for something, it is always advisable to carry only the cash you need. For example, if you are going out with friends for coffee and you had $200 in your envelope for dining out, do not take the entire $200. Just take how much you need to buy coffee. This ensures that you do not overspend and you do not spend all the money allocated for dining out at once.

At the end of the month, check the envelopes to see how much money remains. If you have some leftover, use it to pay off debt or add it to savings. Do not be tempted to spend the money on something you think you missed out on. If you made it through the month without that particular item or treat, then you probably do not need it. Use the money to chip away at your debt, regardless of whether or not you already paid the monthly charge. A debt overpayment goes a long way to prevent fines and penalties. Additionally, saving is a way of ensuring that you do not take on more debt in the future once you have cleared current debts.

Revisit your budget

It is advisable to revisit your budget after two or three months. Each time you will be more aware of your spending patterns and the amount that goes into expenses that had previously not been accounted for, like veterinary bills, home or car repairs. Make the necessary expenditure adjustments but be sure to balance the inflows and outflows. With such adjustments, you should now have a workable and comprehensive budget. While you must stick to the budget, you must also realize that no budget is permanent. With time, you will be done paying off certain debts, leaving you with additional disposable income that you can reallocate to savings or other expenses. Also, if you receive an increase in income or a promotion, it would be wise to increase your savings and debt payments. Alternatively, if you have cleared debts, you can increase your discretionary expenses, but only proportionately to increased savings. On the other hand, if you take a pay cut or are laid off, you must be ready to adjust your budget that way, too.

DEBT ELIMINATION STRATEGIES

So far you have learned how to organize debt payments as you build an emergency fund in a bid to ensure that you do not fall into the debt trap again. Now we'll cover which debt elimination plan is right for you. The debt elimination strategies discussed below are the two most common.

The snowball strategy

The "snowball" strategy requires you to list all your debts in order from smallest to largest. You must list all the debt you have, including mortgages, credit cards, car loans, student loans, payday loans, or any other type, despite its nature or amount. For example, if you have a credit card balance of $500, $1,000, and $2,000; you should list them in that particular order and start the repayment from the smallest loan amount, then the next largest, and so on. The largest loan should be paid last.

The snowball strategy advocates for the dedication of as much money as possible towards the lowest debt balance, as you continue to meet the minimum monthly payment for the other debts. Once the lowest debt is fully repaid, you redirect the money that was dedicated to its repayment towards offsetting the next lowest debt amount as an addition to its minimum monthly payment. Payment of the second lowest balance is a "snowball" because it is a combination of the amount that you used to pay off the first debt in addition to the minimum amount that you have been paying for the second lowest loan. Continue to snowball all debt until you clear them out.

Envision a snowball as it rolls on the ground; it picks up more snow and it gets bigger and bigger. Similarly, every conquered debt frees up more money that you can use to pay off the next debt. This debt elimination strategy is quite popular because it offers a series of small wins that keep debtors motivated to work towards paying off big loans. Moreover, it offers an opportunity to improve your credit rating especially if you choose to pay off the credit card loans first.

Illustration of the snowball strategy

Debt Type	Balance
Credit card loan	$3,000
Auto loan	$10,000
Student loan	$15,000

- Adhere to payment of required monthly minimum amounts for each loan.
- Use any extra money or disposable income towards offsetting the lowest loan, in this case, is the credit card loan.
- Once you have cleared the credit card loan, dedicate the money you were using to repay it towards eliminating the auto loan.
- Once you pay off the auto loan, use the money you have been paying to pay off the student loan.

Pros and cons of the snowball strategy

The snowball debt elimination strategy is effective if you have a number of small debts and if you need the motivation to pay off your debts faster. It may be the best debt elimination strategy if you have multiple outstanding credit card balances, yet you cannot qualify for credit card balance transfer or low-interest debt consolidation loans. When you are deep into the debt trap, this strategy keeps you motivated by offering progress within the shortest time possible. Also, you get peace of mind when you gradually get rid of the lowest loan balances and reduce outstanding balance accounts.

The major disadvantage of the snowball strategy is that you could end up paying more money in the long term since it does not factor in interest rates. As such, the highest interest loan may be paid much later or even last, extra time costs more in regard to interest charges.

The avalanche strategy

Similar to the snowball strategy, the "avalanche" strategy requires you to list all your debts despite their nature or amount. However, you should list the debts by their interest rates, where the debt with the highest interest charges comes first, followed by the second-highest interest rate, and so on. With this strategy, you get rid of the high-interest loans first, ensuring that you pay less interest over time.

You are required to dedicate as much money as possible each month towards paying off the highest interest loan. Once it is paid off, use that money to pay off the debt with the second highest interest rate. Continue in this way until all the loans are paid off. Each time you pay off a loan, you free up extra money that you can dedicate towards paying the next debt in the specified order. Similar to an avalanche, it will take some time before seeing tangible results, but eventually you will witness the debts falling away faster than a rushing snow wall.

Illustration of the avalanche debt elimination strategy

Debt Type	Balance	Intrest Rate
Credit card loan	$3,000	20%
Auto loan	$10,000	5%
Student Loan	$15,000	4%

- Always pay the required minimum monthly repayments for each loan on time.
- Use any extra money to pay off the loan with the highest interest rate, in this case, the credit card loan.
- Once you have paid off the credit card loan,

redirect the money you were using to pay it off towards payment of the next high-interest loan, in this case, the student loan.
- Do the same for the auto loan once the student loan is cleared.

Pros and cons of the debt avalanche strategy

The avalanche debt elimination strategy not only helps you get out of debt faster but also ensures that you pay less interest. Hence, the avalanche strategy is highly recommended for debt elimination, especially among people who are struggling to make payments. It makes a lot of sense to pay off the high-interest loan debts first as a way of saving money in the long term. The major drawback is that it takes time to see tangible results, unlike when applying the snowball strategy.

Choosing between snowball and avalanche strategies

Though any debt elimination strategy that helps you get out of debt is excellent, there is a strategy that resonates with your current financial situation and future plans. So, how do you settle on either the snowball or the avalanche strategy? Start by understanding your personality, defining your current financial position, and future financial goals. The ideal debt elimination strategy is one that falls in line with your way of thinking.

The snowball strategy factors in the behavioral and emotional aspects of personal finance. For most people, money is more than figures; it is how they feel about it. Therefore, it is perfect for people who feel liberated by small wins because it focuses on payment of the lowest debt balances first. As such, you clear your first debt faster and get to enjoy that win, which in turn keeps you motivated to achieve bigger and better personal finance goals like becoming debt-free. It makes all the difference by reducing and eventually eliminating the frustrations associated with debt repayment.

The avalanche strategy may be better than the snowball strategy, mathematically speaking. This is because it focuses on clearing the debt with the highest interest rate first, despite the outstanding balance. This strategy helps you save money in the long term because you reduce the interest you are required to pay. However, if you have a huge balance on the high-interest loan, it will take longer to repay it and see encouraging results as compared to the snowball strategy. If you find it emotionally draining to wait that long for your first debt repayment milestone, you may opt for the snowball strategy.

It is advisable to choose the debt elimination strategy that motivates you. If paying off your first loan faster keeps you hopeful and motivated to work harder towards repaying the remaining debt, choose the snowball strategy. On the other hand, if you are motivated by the fact that you will save money by eliminating high-interest loans first and spare some cash for saving or discretionary expenses, opt for the avalanche strategy.

DEBT CONSOLIDATION

Debt consolidation, also referred to as credit consolidation or bill consolidation, is a great solution for people who are overwhelmed by multiple bank loans and credit cards. This strategy entails merging multiple debts into a single debt, which can then be paid off through a management program or a loan. It reduces monthly payments and interest rates to cut your pending debt costs. As such, it can be an effective solution for offsetting high-interest debt. Debt consolidation untangles the mess debtors face each month as they try to keep up with multiple credit card and loan payment deadlines. Upon consolidation, you are required to make one payment monthly.

Debt consolidation is ideal if it lowers the monthly payments and the overall interest rate, especially for unsecured debt, like credit cards. If you are considering debt consolidation, add up all your monthly payments, and then determine the average interest you pay for them. This provides you with a baseline comparison. The next step is evaluating your monthly budget to determine how much you can afford to dedicate towards loan repayment without straining.

Debt consolidation using a loan

Bank or credit union loans are the conventional debt consolidation method. If you decide to take out a debt consolidation loan, you must approach your bank, credit union, or a non-profit debt consolidation company. However, it is advisable to be very careful when working with a non-profit debt consolidation company because most include extra fees that they may not disclose upfront. In some cases, such hidden fees make the loan more expensive than the cost of your consolidated debt.

Before approaching your bank for a consolidation loan, make sure you know the exact amount you will need to offset all the pending debt. Request your loan and negotiate for the lowest interest rate possible. In most cases, the consolidation loan repayment period ranges between three to five years, but it is the interest that is a key element in determining the cumulative loan amount and duration. Consolidation loans are fixed interest loans with fixed monthly payments. The interest rate you are charged depends on your current credit rating. So if you have been falling behind on your credit card payments, it is highly likely that your consolidation loan provider will offer a slightly higher interest rate.

Note, if the debt consolidation loan interest rate you are offered is not lower than the average interest rate of your outstanding debts, then it is not worth taking. In that event, it would be advisable to seek alternative loans, like a personal loan or a home equity loan. However, neither would be of help if the offered interest rate is still higher or the repayment period is longer.

It is important to understand that consolidation loans do not eliminate debt; instead, they restructure multiple debts into a single loan with more favorable terms that you can pay with ease. As such, it makes sense to compare debt consolidation loan offers before settling for an initial offer. Shopping around can increase your chances of getting a better offer or interest rate.

Secured versus unsecured debt consolidation loans

Debt consolidation loans are more or less personal loans that are categorized as either secured or unsecured. A secured consolidation loan is supported by collateral like your home, property, or car. On the other hand, an unsecured loan is supported by your promise to repay the loan as agreed. As such, unsecured loans may attract higher interest rates as compared to secured loans. Moreover, secured loans are easy to obtain, offer high amounts and lower interest charges that may also be tax-deductible. They do tend to have longer repayment periods (that eventually translate to more cumulative interest paid) and you bear the risk of losing your collateral should you default on the loan. Unsecured loans have shorter payment terms that translate to a lower amount paid since you pay less interest over time. Additionally, you do not risk losing your collateral. Unsecured loans are hard to obtain, attract high-interest charges, have no tax benefits, and offer a lower principle amount that in some cases may not be enough to offset your outstanding debts.

Types of debt consolidation loans

There are four main types of debt consolidation loans. They include credit card balance transfers, home equity loans, unsecured debt consolidation, and personal loans from friends and family.

Home equity loans: If you have home equity, a home equity loan for debt consolidation would be your best bet. This is because home equity loans have substantially less interest charged as compared to other types of debt consolidation loans. However, your home's equity amount determines the amount you can borrow.

Credit card balance transfers: This type of debt consolidation is ideal for people who have multiple high-interest credit card balances. In most cases, you can negotiate a zero-interest credit card balance transfer, transfer all your credit card balances, and then pay them off with no interest within 6 to 24 months. However, to qualify for a zero-interest balance transfer you must have an excellent credit rating. Additionally, most credit card companies charge a balance transfer fee of 2 to 3 percent of the outstanding balances, which could add up to a sizable amount. Also, you are required to repay the entire transferred amount within the given time frame; otherwise, the regular credit card interest rate will apply.

Unsecured loans: Interest costs for unsecured loans are based on your credit score. They are a good option for people who are deep in debt and do not have a valuable asset that they can offer lenders as collateral.

Loans from friends and family: If you are lucky enough to have financially stable friends and family members, this could be the best debt consolidation option because the interest rates and terms of repayment are flexible. It is easy to change payment terms to accommodate a change in your income. However, you risk losing trust or friendships should you fail to honor your repayment as agreed.

Debt consolidation without a loan

As aforementioned, it is possible to consolidate debt through a debt management program if you do not qualify for a debt consolidation loan. A debt management program is ideal for people who do not have a strong credit score. Credit counseling agencies offer non-profit debt consolidation options that do not require debtors to take out loans. Instead, they work with your credit card companies or financial institutions to lower your monthly payments and interest rates to more affordable rates based on your income level. They also negotiate with creditors to waive the limit and late payment charges.

Once you reach an agreement with the credit counseling agency, you are required to send a predetermined amount of money every month to them. The agency then distributes the agreed-upon payment amounts to the creditors. Conversely, debt management programs take about three to five years to eliminate debt, based on your outstanding balance. Should you default on monthly payments, the credit counseling agency can revoke any concessions that they had offered on your monthly payments and interest rates.

Does debt consolidation affect credit score?

If used appropriately within a personal finance plan, debt

consolidation offers an opportunity to redeem and improve your credit score. When you take out a debt consolidation loan, you pay off all the credit card or bank loans you had in full and focus only on paying a single loan. Opting for debt consolidation means that you may have been struggling to make multiple loan repayments and chances are high that your credit rating has been negatively affected by delinquent payments. But, if you have negotiated a lower interest rate and flexible monthly payments based on your income, it will be a lot easier to pay down the consolidation loan. Making timely payments on the consolidation loan will impact your credit score positively. As such, you must make the loan a top financial priority. Do not take on other financial responsibilities or fall for credit card promotions that only incur additional debt.

DEBT SETTLEMENT

Debt settlement is a legal debt elimination strategy whereby a debtor negotiates with creditors, preferably through a debt settlement company, to pay less than the amount owed. It is considered a viable debt approach, especially compared to bankruptcy. The main aim of debt settlement is to enable the debtor to pay significantly less than the outstanding balance. Though it is possible to negotiate a debt settlement yourself, it is advisable to work with a long-standing debt settlement company that has the experience and know-how to drive a hard bargain. Additionally, creditors and debt collection agencies are fond of using intimidating tactics in a bid to scare debtors into paying the full amount owed. On the other hand, debt settlement companies have handled different debt cases and know the right strategies to get creditors and debt collection agencies to accept an affordable debt settlement. This way, you get an opportunity to start over and save the money you could have spent paying interest and penalties.

Debt settlement companies are not only experienced at negotiating with creditors but also have good relationships with major credit card and financial institutions. Conversely, they hire credit counselors who are experienced and accredited to review personal finances and offer the best advice possible on how to get out of debt through settlement. Also, they have a keen understanding of current economic and market trends that determine why and how creditors will negotiate a settlement. Hence, your best bet would be working with a settlement company.

Once you approach a debt settlement company, you are assigned a credit counselor who evaluates your current financial situation vis-à-vis your outstanding debt amount and uses the information to design an ideal settlement plan. The settlement plan explains in detail the monthly payment plan and how the settlement company benefits.

There is a caveat; it takes about 36 to 48 months for a debtor to save enough money before the debt settlement company can bargain for a competitive offer. During that period, the late and default payment penalties and interest can accumulate to alarming amounts. Moreover, once the debt is settled, the settlement is recorded in your credit account as an indication that the debts were not paid in full. Meaning your credit report and score are stained for roughly seven years after such an event. The next time you opt to take out a loan, your creditor will know that your previous debts were settled and that may compromise your ability to access good lines of credit.

How debt settlement works

Once you decide to eliminate your debts through debt

settlement, the first step should be deciding whether to work with a lawyer or a debt settlement company. Remember that experience is key. If you choose to work with a lawyer ensure that they have handled debt settlement cases before. The goal is to reduce the payable amount significantly and typically only an experienced lawyer can achieve that. Also, you must have enough money to make an offer that the creditors will not turn down, so if this is your plan, you should start saving immediately.

The next step is meeting with your creditors to get them to accept a settlement. If you had defaulted on payments for more than six months, your debt may have been transferred to a debt collection agency, whose sole aim is to get as much money as possible. If that is the case, it would be harder, but not impossible, to negotiate for a settlement.

Depending on your outstanding debt amount, it could take up to three or four years to save enough money for a settlement offer. Your debt settlement representative will advise you to stop making your regular monthly payments and instead build a settlement account by putting that money in an escrow account they provide. As you do this, your interest and debt balances grow.

Once you have saved enough money and it is time to approach the creditors for an offer, you must be very patient because creditors are not obligated to accept debt settlement offers. As such, the process may take months or even years before a deal is made. Once the creditor accepts your offer, you are required to have it in writing and the creditor is obligated to notify all credit bureaus that the debt is settled.

Though better than bankruptcy, debt settlement comes at a cost. If you work with a debt settlement company, expect to pay 15% of the outstanding debt amount or 25% of the total saved amount. If you work with a lawyer, expect to pay a standard fee or an hourly rate. In addition, there are tax charges paid to the IRS for the forgiven debt amount.

BANKRUPTCY

Bankruptcy is a court proceeding where a court trustee or judge examines a debtor's assets and liabilities to decide whether or not their outstanding debts can be discharged so that they are no longer legally obligated to pay them. Bankruptcy laws were created to give people in financial turmoil the chance to start over. Whether a person gets in financial distress as a result of bad luck or poor decision making, lawmakers understood that everyone deserves a second chance, especially in a capitalistic economy.

For an individual to file for bankruptcy they must have huge debts that they cannot clear under their current financial situation and they do not expect a change anytime soon. For instance, as of 2019, bankruptcy filers had $116 billion in debts and their assets were valued at $83.6 billion, most of which were real estate holdings with debatable values. Unfortunately, it is not hard to find yourself in a place where you need to file for bankruptcy, especially if you have a lot of high-interest debt like student loans, auto loans, credit cards, or mortgages, yet you do not have a stable income.

There is no perfect time to file for bankruptcy but if you are struggling to keep up with your monthly payments and you expect to repay all your debt in not less than five years, declaring bankruptcy may be the ideal move. Keep in mind that bankruptcy was designed to give people a second chance to make better financial choices. Therefore, if you are overwhelmed by loans, you do not have an income, and you do not expect things to change in the near future, declaring bankruptcy will give you the peace of mind and emotional relief you need to sail through the financial turmoil.

Remember, bankruptcy has a devastating effect on your credit score. Bankruptcy declaration remains on the credit report for up to ten years. On the bright side, it delays or prevents foreclosure on your home, car repossession, prevents wage garnishment and use of legal actions by creditors. In legal terms, bankruptcy is referred to as "the automatic stay." Meaning that creditors are barred from filing any lawsuit against you, constantly contacting you for debt payments, or entering liens against your assets. It also prevents eviction and disconnection of utilities.

Filing for bankruptcy

If you reach the conclusion that bankruptcy is the best option you have, you must compile your financial records including your assets, income, expenses, and debts. This gives you and the court a better understanding of your current financial position. Before filing for bankruptcy, you are required to receive credit counseling at least 180 days prior to initiating the process. Note that you must enroll for counseling with an approved credit counseling provider who must be listed on the United States Courts website. In most cases, the counseling services are offered over the phone or online.

Credit counseling is a mandatory step because the courts want to ensure that you fully understand other debt elimination options available before filing for bankruptcy. Once you complete credit counseling, a certificate of completion must be awarded and attached as part of your bankruptcy paperwork. Failure to attach the bankruptcy certificate leads to rejection of your petition.

After acquiring a certificate of completion, the next step is filing your bankruptcy petition. At this point, you either need to hire a lawyer or you can choose to represent yourself (though the latter would be high risk). This is because you may not fully understand the state and federal bankruptcy laws that apply to your case in regard to the nature of debts that can and cannot be discharged. However, legal representation is not mandatory when filing for Chapter 7 or Chapter 13 bankruptcies. Nonetheless, there are numerous forms that must be completed and Chapter 7 and Chapter 13 bankruptcies have crucial differences that an applicant must be aware of to ensure that they make the right decision. Failure to adhere to court rules and the bankruptcy petition procedures could affect the petition's outcome. Free legal services may be provided if you cannot afford to hire a lawyer.

In the event that your petition is accepted, the case is transferred to a court trustee who initiates the property dissolution procedure by inviting all creditors for a meeting. It is mandatory for you to attend the meeting but creditors are not obligated to attend. The meeting gives creditors a chance to ask you and the court trustee questions about the case as well decide how the asset liquidation will be carried out.

Types of bankruptcy

Chapter 7 bankruptcy: This type of bankruptcy releases a debtor from the responsibilities of debt repayment. It permits the retention of key assets that are classified as exempt properties. However, non-exempt properties are liquidated to pay off part of the outstanding debt. Since property exemptions vary from one state to another, you are allowed to follow either the federal or state laws based on the law that allows retention of more property.

Exempt properties include a home, a car used for work, work equipment, pensions, social security checks, retirement savings, welfare, and veterans benefits, among others. Such properties cannot be liquidated to pay off debt. Non-exempt properties include bank accounts, cash, stamp or coin collections, stock investments, a second home, or a second car, among others. Non-exempt properties are liquidated and the proceeds are used to pay down debt. Note, the non-exempt properties are sold by a court trustee assigned to your case and the proceeds are divided to pay the trustee, administrative fees, and creditors respectively.

Chapter 13 bankruptcy: This type of bankruptcy is characterized by payment of some debts in a bid to have others forgiven. It is ideal for people who do not qualify for Chapter 7 bankruptcy because they have high income levels yet they are not willing to give up their property. Debtors are allowed to file for Chapter 13 bankruptcy if their debt amount does not exceed a legally predetermined amount that is evaluated occasionally. Therefore, you must consult with your lawyer or credit counselor for updated cutoff figures.

Under the Chapter 13 bankruptcy act, the debtor is required to design a three to five year debt repayment plan for their chosen creditors. Upon successful completion of the repayment plan, the remaining debts are forgiven. Unfortunately, not very many people who opt for this type of bankruptcy petition have their plans agreed upon. When a debtor is unable to honor the agreed debt payment plan, they are allowed to pursue Chapter 7 bankruptcy. Otherwise, creditors are allowed to claim payment of outstanding debt balances in full.

Effects of bankruptcy

The main benefit of filing a bankruptcy petition is that you get a fresh financial start. Though it will impact your credit rating negatively, you will enjoy mental and emotional freedom by being debt-free. Chapter 7 bankruptcy remains on your credit report for ten years while Chapter 13 is listed for seven years. During the time when bankruptcy is listed on your credit report, it may be hard to secure new credit lines and in some cases a job.

If you are considering bankruptcy as a debt elimination strategy, chances are high that your credit score and report are already damaged. Therefore, the damage cannot get much worse than it already is, especially if you pay your bills consistently after a bankruptcy declaration. However, according to financial experts, the long-term bankruptcy effects are not worth it if your debts are less than $15,000. Keep in mind that bankruptcy does not protect your debt co-signers. They may be required to pay off your debts in part or in full even after you are declared bankrupt.

Chapter Summary

- Engaging creditors is a good way to ensure that your debt situation doesn't get out of hand if you are unable to honor monthly payments.
- A budget curbs overspending and helps you keep tabs on how you spend your money.
- Common debt elimination strategies include debt consolidation, debt settlement, the snowball strategy, the avalanche strategy, and filing for bankruptcy. Choose one based on your financial situation.

CHAPTER FIVE: STAYING OUT OF DEBT

At this point, you have probably made progress towards paying off your debt. You are on the right path to finally be in control of your finances. Soon you will be debt-free, stress-free, and able to build wealth. Moreover, you are bound to feel happier and more confident about yourself upon repaying all debts. If your self-esteem was dented, it will increase and you will be thrilled to take on bigger financial responsibilities. In as much as people love fitting in certain societal classes through spending beyond their means, we cannot deny the fact that we all long for financial stability, wealth creation, and above all, self-actualization. The first step to achieving such personal finance goals is eliminating debt and staying out of debt. But, it is easier said than done!

Once you clear all your debt and have extra disposable income, it is easy to fall back to the poor spending habits that got you into debt in the first place. The relief you feel after paying off all your debt is likened to the acquisition of freedom after being held down in an unfavorable situation. This feeling can easily drive you to make poor money decisions. For instance, you may think of rewarding yourself with a better car or a dream vacation. Self-rewarding is not wrong; in fact, it is advisable to reward yourself after overcoming the debt trap. However, going overboard by purchasing things you cannot afford does more damage than good since you will slowly fall back into debt without realizing it.

As discussed in the previous chapters, it is highly likely that you had to make financial adjustments in order to cut down spending. For example, you may have moved to a more affordable house, sold your expensive car for a more affordable one, or reduced social meet-ups with friends. Whatever adjustment or sacrifice you made was worth it because it helped you get out of debt. According to personal finance experts, it is best to remain in the same position as you were when paying off debt. Do not be tempted to upgrade to a different lifestyle because you have extra money to spend. Instead, reintroduce the things you deem necessary yet affordable, and focus on building a strong emergency fund that will help you avoid debt in the future. For example, you may reintroduce dining out, vacations, or hang out with friends more often without overspending.

To ensure that you do not overspend as you reintroduce such activities, start by reevaluating your budget. Let's refer to the envelope-style budgeting where you have different envelopes for your different monthly expenses. Assuming that your utilities remain consistent, you may add a little extra cash to the groceries or discretionary expenses envelopes. Dining out or hanging out with friends should be paid off the discretionary expenses envelope and once it runs out of cash, you stop spending on discretionary expenses. You stick to a budget, avoid getting into debt, and above all, remain in control of your finances. To stay out of debt you need:

Financial Discipline

Financial discipline means living within your means, resisting the urge to spend on unnecessary things that are not within your budget, sticking to your budget, and above all, having adequate savings that are only used during an emergency. Like any other form of discipline, financial discipline can be enforced through motivation or punishment. In this case, you have attained or are forced to attain financial discipline through punishment as you pay down debt and through motivation after you clear all debts.

Poor financial choices led you into the debt trap that you struggled so hard to get out of, you had to make extreme sacrifices in order to pay off debt and gain full control of your money. That is punishment. Fortunately, discipline is dubbed punishment at the beginning but it later triggers motivation once you have good results. To maintain financial discipline, you must abide by the basic rules of spending, borrowing, saving, and investing as described in the previous chapters.

The main cause of financial problems is a lack of financial discipline and self-control. Most people lack the ability to delay instant or short-term gratification they get by dining out, buying the latest designer outfit, buying an expensive car, a big house, going on vacations, holding house parties, or buying the latest phone. The inability to delay gratification pushes you to spend all your income and supplement any expense deficit with credit cards or loans. You will gradually, but surely, pay dearly for them through high-interest rates and personal financial instability. Unfortunately, this happens because many Americans link happiness to spending.

Therefore, achieving financial discipline should start with rewiring the mind and your perceptions about money. Start linking happiness to saving, investing, being debt-free, and having a good emergency fund that you can fall back on when things get tough. The importance of saving and having an emergency fund has been well explained in the previous chapter. Just to recap, start building your emergency fund with the little money you are left with after paying your monthly payments. Stick to the saving pattern every month and with time it will become a habit. Moreover, your self-awareness and your self-esteem grow as your emergency fund grows. With time, you are bound to feel happier about yourself and your financial choices since you will have the means to build wealth without being financially dependent on banks or credit card companies. Additionally, the money in your savings account creates an energy force field that attracts more money. As the saying goes, "it takes money to make money." As you build your emergency fund month after month, the universe has a way of directing more money your way to save and create wealth. The universal rule of financial independence is paying yourself first before spending. This means that you should start with saving and budget for what is left.

Increased Monthly Savings

As aforementioned, saving to build a strong emergency fund ought to be your core goal upon getting out of debt. If you have just started saving, it is possible to get comfortable setting aside just a small percentage of your income, as was the case when paying off debt. You never saved anything before, yet you survived, so why hold back on enjoying life now that you are debt-free and have more money to spend on luxuries? This is the grave thought that pulls people back into debt, especially young Americans who believe they can focus on wealth creation later in life. Unfortunately, if you do not plan your finances while young, it will be hard to keep up with the ever-increasing financial responsibilities as you age.

Therefore, make saving a habit and increase the amount you save every month as your income increases. In the event you have cleared all debt balances, redirect the money you used to pay off debts each month towards savings instead. This is the best way to build a strong emergency fund faster. For instance, if you were saving 10% of your income while using 20% to pay off debts, it would be in your best interest to increase the savings to at least 25% once you are debt-free. Depending on your income, 25% may not be much but in one year, you will have accumulated an equivalent of 25% of your annual income. If you maintain the same trend, you should have 50% of your annual salary in savings by the end of the second year.

Also, ensure that you save any monetary windfalls, like cash gifts, tax refunds, work bonuses, or any other cash sources that are not included in your budget. Each time you get a cash infusion, direct it strictly to savings. The logic behind this is that if you have been surviving on $2,000 monthly you will not need an extra $1,000 to get through the month. So, save the extra money you get, unless you are faced with an emergency that was not budgeted for.

In order to uphold good savings habits and save as much as possible, it is advisable to live below your means. Though this means having to make sacrifices and probably denying yourself instant gratification, it is a small price to pay when you are determined to achieve financial stability and above all, stay out of debt. It is upon you to practice financial discipline by not taking out debt to pay for things you can live without or adopting an expensive lifestyle.

Have Targeted Savings Accounts

By now I am sure you understand the importance of saving and you are slowly building an emergency fund. However, in order to ensure that your emergency savings are reserved for emergencies, it is important to have targeted savings accounts. Without targeted savings accounts, you are highly likely to raid your emergency fund for big purchases. Targeted savings accounts are regular savings accounts that are geared towards specific financial goals. They are the perfect place to stash money for big purchases like buying a car, a home, or a dream vacation.

Though most people may not like the idea of having multiple savings accounts, they help you keep track of your progress towards specific saving goals. On the contrary, a single savings account may make it hard for you to tell whether you have achieved your goals. For instance, if you are saving for a car and a vacation simultaneously in just a single account, it would be hard to determine whether you have saved enough for either the car or the vacation, or both. You lose track of how much money is saved for each goal. Moreover, it would be easy to run down the savings account as you fulfill either of the two goals and end up compromising the other. This is because fuzzy savings goals rarely pay off.

Needless to say, targeted savings accounts trigger good money habits because you will have more reasons to monitor your spending and money goals. However, before you embark on your different savings goals, it is important to have a strong financial foundation. It is advisable to have at least 6 months of your salary in savings. Also, it is best to start with one targeted savings account to get a feel for the idea. For example, if you want to buy another car, open a savings account, and name it accordingly. Determine the amount you will be saving, based on your income level. If your income is inconsistent, set a reasonable amount that you can afford (even in the toughest month!) and when earning more, save extra. Commit to that single plan and once you are comfortable with the idea, add more savings accounts as per your personal goals. The trick is to start small and grow gradually.

Make Realistic Personal Lifestyle Choices

Personal lifestyle choices determine how much you spend, save, and above all, whether you fall into the debt trap or stay out of debt. There are many things that you can do differently to improve your financial situation and never have to worry about managing your finances, taking out huge loans, or struggling to pay them off. Things like education, weddings, and buying a car are unavoidable, but if not managed realistically, they may set you on the wrong financial path as explained below.

Education

On average, most Americans graduate with student debt of around $30,000 from a four-year college. This is a huge debt for a young graduate considering the entry-level income levels and the cost of living. However, according to a report by the Association of Public & Land Grant Universities, a third of four-year college graduates leave school debt-free. Though some of these students may have rich parents or relatives who cover their education; there are some who manage to graduate debt-free without much help from family. How do these students manage to graduate debt-free yet the cost of university education in America is so high? They apply some of the following strategies.

Attend community college

The annual average cost of tuition in a four-year public university is $10,500 and $3,700 in a community college. With these figures in mind, it would be more realistic to start off at a two-year community college to save money and avoid large student loans. Though this is a tough decision for most students and parents because we all want the best, it is important to think about your personal or your family's financial future upon graduating with a hefty student loan that none of you can afford to pay.

You can complete your general course requirements at an affordable community college and later transfer to a four-year college for your degree. However, it is important to make sure that the credits earned at a community college are transferable to a four-year college, and that they will count towards your degree. Start your associate's degree journey by signing up for a transfer program at your chosen community college just to be sure that your strategy pays off.

Some people may argue that the quality of education offered in certain highly ranked four-year universities is better than that of community colleges. However, the programs offered in two-year colleges are similar to the programs offered in the first two years of study at four-year colleges. Moreover, associate's degrees are specially designed to ensure that students make easy transitions into universities upon graduation.

If you plan on entering a four-year college after earning your associate's degree, ensure that you save as you learn. If possible, stay at home to minimize costs, get a part-time job, and open a tuition savings account. It is possible to save a year's worth of tuition fees within the two years while studying at a community college. Additionally, upon acquisition of an associate's degree, you will probably get a higher paying job. This will only make it easier for you to pay for your degree and graduate debt-free.

Applying for scholarships and grants

The mere thought of having to go through the daunting scholarship application process without a guarantee of actually receiving anything discourages a lot of students. But getting free money to pay for college is one way of ensuring that you stay out of debt. Basically, the work involved up front is a small price to pay. The best way to get college scholarships and grants are by looking into local offers. There are numerous universities and community colleges that offer grants and substantial scholarships to local students. The good news is that such offers have less competition compared to other scholarship offers. Start the search at your school guidance office; local organizations and businesses pitch their offers to local schools and colleges.

Buying a second-hand car

As cars become more expensive, the interest rates are rising, and hence, longer and more expensive auto loans. The average cost of a new car is $32,000 while the average interest cost of an auto loan is $5,500. Not to mention the pay duration may be more than five years. This is a huge price to pay for a car whose value will reduce to less than half the initial cost by the time you are done paying off the loan. It would be in your best interest to opt for a second-hand car instead.

Though the average age of a car on the road is twelve, most cars depreciate to half their original value in only three years. It is possible to get a good second-hand car of your choice at a lower price and loan if you will rely on asset financing. However, it is advisable to vet the history of your preferred second-hand car thoroughly before buying. Use the car identification number to check its history with the National Motor Vehicle Title Information Center and any other organization that stores a vehicle's history. Keep an eye out for vehicle buying incentives that could help in saving money through offers such as; cash-back deals and zero percent interest rates.

Opt for a more simple wedding

Weddings are a once in a lifetime event, used to signify a major commitment between two consenting adults and the start of a new phase in life. Due to the importance of the event, couples tend to overspend on their big day, forgetting that they need a strong financial foundation to build a family. The estimated average cost of a wedding in the United States is $30,000. Unfortunately, most couples cannot afford to foot such an expense without taking on debt, and here is where the problem sets in. Imagine starting your marriage with such a hefty debt that you will be paying for it for years.

72% percent of wedding debtors noted that they could have held more simple weddings that would not have incurred debt, while 37% regret getting into debt to finance a one-day event. This is an indication that the amount you spend to finance your wedding is solely up to you. You can choose to go all out and pay for the big day over a couple of years or avoid getting into debt by holding a simple wedding. After all, all you want is to get married to the love of your life and build a meaningful and stress-free life together.

Most couples get into debt to finance their weddings because they have set certain expectations or feel pressured to have a big, spectacular wedding. Though these reasons are valid, it is important to consider whether all the debt-inducing ideas are really worthy. Must you have so many guests? Must every guest have an ice cream bar? Focus on the basic wedding necessities like a good venue, enough chairs for your guests, and of course, a professionally baked cake. If you have some money left over after paying for basic necessities, add in a few extras that would make your wedding as lavish as you would want without going overboard.

With a huge wedding loan, you start off your union on the wrong foot, especially considering that you probably have other debts like car or student loans. Don't add another financial burden that will not boost your earning potential or wealth as a couple. The money you would have used to pay off the wedding debt can be used to save and pay for your dream home.

Chapter Summary

- The best way to stay out of debt is to live within your means and build an emergency fund that you can fall back on when things get tough.
- Make realistic financial decisions such as opting for a second-hand car, a simpler wedding, and less expensive education options.
- Above all, uphold financial discipline.

CHAPTER SIX: BUILDING YOUR WEALTH

Now that you have managed to pay all your debts and mastered the art of staying out debt, it is time to start building wealth. Building wealth ensures that you are able to maintain your living standard, even after losing your main source of income. Above all, wealth creation guarantees a healthy and stress-free retirement. Imagine having multiple sources of passive income and no debt upon retirement. That is what we all hope to achieve but we fail to plan and make the necessary lifestyle adjustments when we can. Here are a few things you can do to start your wealth creation journey when still young.

HOW TO BUILD WEALTH

Invest in education

Though this may not be an ideal wealth creation strategy for many, investing in education, especially for young people, is the best way to increase your disposable income. Investing in education could be acquiring a degree, certification, or switching to a more marketable career if you are not comfortable with your current pay. For instance, a good number of people have switched from different career fields to nursing because it is marketable and the pay is fairly good. Moreover, in order to earn more, you must stand out from the competition by having something unique, such as a skill or extra certification. You may be surprised how the acquisition of an extra certification in your career field can yield thousands of dollars in income over the years. This is extra money that you can invest wisely to build wealth.

Work hard now

Hard work pays; this is a phrase that is used a lot yet rarely actualized. Before you acquire financial freedom, you will have to rely on employment and the income you earn to create wealth. Despite the nature of your job, it is always advisable to work hard. Give your job all you have, because that is what keeps you afloat. Putting in the hard work sets you up so you are bound to get better work or investment opportunities. For example, if you have just graduated and the best work offer you got was an internship, give the internship your all and work hard to impress. Always get to work on time, dress professionally, and be ready to work. Even when you are not offered a full-time position, you will definitely get a good recommendation that will set you apart from the competition when interviewing for your next job. Furthermore, when economic calamity strikes and the company is forced to lay off employees to mitigate costs, chances are high that your job will be safe. Employers will always opt to keep the most dedicated, reliable, and hardworking employees they have. Do not forget that your main aim is to gather resources and build wealth. Therefore, scout for entrepreneurship opportunities in line with your career or other opportunities that would generate additional income without compromising your productivity at work. Should you opt to quit your job for entrepreneurship, ensure that you have enough saved in your emergency account to avoid falling into the debt trap.

Increase retirement contributions

It is highly likely that you slowed down or halted retirement contributions while paying off debt, which was a good move. Now that you are debt-free though, you should work on building your retirement contributions. Review your budget and determine the amount you can contribute towards retirement. You can increase the contribution based on the level of your disposable income or set aside the recommended 15% of your income. If your employer offers a 401(K) program, be sure to contribute at least the required minimum. If your employer matches any amount contributed to the plan, contribute a sizable amount because you will essentially be getting free money from your employer. Once you max it out, you can open another retirement contribution account like a Roth IRA or a traditional IRA. Conversely, always increase your retirement contribution as your income increases. After all, it is money that you put aside to ensure that you have a stable financial future when your energy to work is run down.

Start investing

One of the common myths about investing that holds people back is the belief that you must have a lot of money to begin. Others just do not know where to start. The key to building wealth through investments is upholding good money habits as discussed in previous chapters. Moreover, starting your investment journey early is the best way to see viable results since your investment will earn compound interest over time.

Note that saving and investing go hand in hand because you must save to get some good investment capital. Start building your investment fund with whatever money you are able to set aside. For instance, if you start with just $50 per month, you will have $600 in one year, which is a substantial amount for investment. Increase the amount as you get comfortable with the process and as your income increases. How much you save for investment should be determined by your investment goal and how fast you need to attain it. Define your investment timeline and amount, then work backward by dividing the amount into weekly or monthly saving goals.

INVESTMENT OPTIONS

Before you invest, it is important to understand your options and their risks. Some of the common investment options that do not require much capital include:

Stock market

Stocks are purchased at the current price per share that can range from a few dollars to thousands of dollars depending on a company's value. The stock market is a great way of building long-term wealth. The trick is investing during periods of market volatility; this is when many stocks are on sale at a lower than normal price. Based on your knowledge about the stock market, you can opt to choose the ideal stock funds yourself or seek guidance from a stock market guru. The latter is advised for beginners. Once you choose your preferred stock investment option, the next step is opening an investment account, better known as a brokerage account. Note, you are allowed to open an investment account with little money and add as you go.

Once your stock investment account is set up, the next step is choosing between stocks and stock mutual funds. Stock mutual funds, also referred to as equity mutual funds, allow you to invest in different stocks through a single transaction. This way, you own minimal shares in each of the companies, making it a great way of mitigating risk. Individual stocks are ideal for people who are interested in a specific company. Unlike stock mutual funds, with individual stocks, you own a small portion of the particular company. It is advisable to build a diversified individual stock portfolio by purchasing individual stocks in different companies as a means of risk mitigation. You can start with just a few shares as you test the waters and purchase more once you get accustomed to stock trading markets and trends.

Since stock mutual funds are diversified and have lower investment risk, they are ideal for people who are investing towards retirement. On the other hand, individual stocks are quite risky but they pay off handsomely if you make a wise and informed pick. You should opt for individual stocks only when you are sure about a company's potential to grow long-term.

Bonds

Bonds are loans given to government entities or companies that agree to pay individuals back with interest after a predetermined period. Bonds are not as risky as stocks since you know the amount you will earn and when you will be paid. As a matter of fact, most financial advisers recommend investing a portion of your money in bonds because they are less volatile and safer than compared to stocks. However, investing in bonds may be tricky because the initial investment amount is determined by the company or government entity. The average face value of bonds is $1,000.

Bonds can be purchased through a broker, an exchange-traded fund, or directly from a government entity. If investing in private company bonds, do your research to determine whether the company has enough financial resources to pay back the lent money with interest. Government bonds are a safe investment option that is ideal for risk-averse investors.

Mutual funds

Mutual funds are investment vehicles consisting of a pool of money that is collected from a wide range of investors. The pool of money is used for investment in money markets, bonds, stocks, and other assets. They are designed to offer investment diversification at an affordable cost. Mutual funds are managed by professional money managers whose duty is producing capital gains and income for the investors. Investors can opt for an actively or passively managed fund. Mutual funds generate income through stock dividends, interest on bonds held on a portfolio, and capital gains. Fund managers distribute the earned income annually to the investors. However, investors are given the option of either reinvesting or withdrawing their gains. Should the value of fund holdings increase in price, the fund's price per share also increases. Therefore, you can sell your mutual fund shares for a profit.

Exchange-traded funds

Exchange-traded funds entail the collection of investment securities like stocks, bonds, and commodities that track an underlying index but they use different investment strategies among different industrial sectors. They are similar to mutual funds with the main difference being that they are listed on exchanges and traded like regular shares. ETFs are marketable securities because they have an associated price that facilitates easy selling and buying. They are purchased through an investment broker. Since ETFs are a pool of different investment measures, they are less risky and investors can be almost sure that their investment will not take losses. This is because when a single stock is performing poorly, another could be doing exceptionally well, thus mitigating the losses and risk of losing the invested principal amount. However, be sure you understand the ETFs objective before investing. Is the fund designed to achieve growth over income? Also, check the bonds and stocks that are in the ETF. Such information helps you determine whether a particular ETF is the ideal investment option for you based on your future plans.

Real estate

Real estate can be a great and lucrative investment if done right. It entails buying and selling buildings and land with the aim of making profits. There are different types of real estates that include residential properties, commercial properties, and industrial properties. Residential properties are apartments, houses, and vacation properties; they are the easiest and most common type of real estate investment among beginners. Commercial properties are buildings that are rented out to businesses such as retail storefronts and office spaces. Industrial properties are storage units, warehouses, and large special-purpose spaces like tow centers and car washes that generate sales.

The main benefit of investing in real estate is consistent cash flow in the form of monthly income. Real estate income is what an investor makes after deducting expenses like management fees, taxes, and insurance. Rental income increases over time as the property appreciates and as inflation increases. Real estate markets can perform exceptionally well even as other investment options don't, due to inflation and other economic factors. Hence, it is the ideal investment for creating consistent passive income and ultimately, building wealth.

TYPES OF REAL ESTATE INVESTMENTS

Rental properties

As long as you can find tenants or purchase a rental property within an area where rental properties are on-demand, residential properties guarantee monthly income all year. Hence, they are the most common type of real estate investment for both beginner and veteran investors. You can opt for industrial and commercial properties too, but their initial purchase costs are quite high as compared to residential properties. However, residential properties require active involvement in regard to building maintenance and management, so most investors opt to contract management companies at an extra cost.

Before purchasing a residential property, ensure that you research and learn about the local real estate market, and understand the neighborhood and the average rental prices. Such information helps you to make informed purchases and offer competitive prices in a bid to ensure that you always have tenants and an income.

CHAPTER SIX: BUILDING YOUR WEALTH

Real estate investment trusts (REITs)

REIT investment is quite common to stock investment because it allows you to invest in real estate without having a physical property. Investors give money to corporations or trusts that in turn purchase real estate properties and manage them. At the end of a trading period, investors are offered dividends that increase as the value of properties appreciate. Note, REITs are purchased and sold on major stock exchanges.

Apart from residential properties, REITs are the easiest way of investing in real estate for beginners that offer high yields. Corporations and trusts pay up to 90% of the property income to investors and the investment can be liquidated at will. You simply sell your shares and cash out without having to advertise or renovate a property to increase its sale value.

Crowdfunding platforms

Just like REITs, crowdfunding platforms are passive real estate investment options. The only difference is that an investor does not go through a corporation or trust. Investors pool together their assets and connect with like-minded developers who need funding for their real estate projects via crowdfunding platforms. Upon funding real estate developers, investors should expect to receive monthly or quarterly payments based on the investment agreement. However, crowdfunding investments are illiquid meaning that they cannot be disposed of with ease. Liquidating your investment depends on market variables making them quite risky as compared to REITs. Note, you might have to wait for long before gaining substantial returns on investment.

Vacation and short-term rentals

If you do not want to buy rental stocks or you do not have enough money to purchase a rental property, short-term and vacation rentals could be a good option for you. If you have an extra room that you do not use, you could rent it out on a weekly or nightly basis. It is also possible to rent out an entire home for short periods. This works best in areas with high tourism traffic. However, you will have to invest in furnishing the space to modern standards in order to get good returns. It is easier to go through websites like Airbnb that connect short-term rental owners with interested parties, mainly tourists who may not be willing to pay the high hotel accommodation costs. Ensure that you review your local laws and regulations that govern short-term and vacation rentals beforehand.

Flip real estate

This option is ideal for investors who are ambitious and willing to undertake construction projects. It entails buying undervalued or dilapidated properties, renovating them, and later selling them at a higher price. Also, you could buy properties for speculation and sell them off once their prices appreciate. However, the properties must be in good enough condition so that you will not have to spend extra money on renovations.

There is an inherent demand for real estate; therefore it will always be a great investment. Real estate gives you the freedom to protect your wealth and future financial stability because it rarely fluctuates in value as compared to the stock market.

CHAPTER SIX: BUILDING YOUR WEALTH

Utilize good debt

As explained in the first chapter, good debt is debt that helps you build wealth because it helps you achieve your set objectives. For instance, student loans are good debt because they help you earn a degree or qualification and higher income. Another type of good debt is taking out a mortgage to purchase a rental property or a loan to finance a realistic business idea. Use good debt to grow your net worth by investing in cash-flowing assets. However, sometimes a good debt can turn out to be bad if taken without a clear objective in place.

In this case, you could use good debt to invest in real estate. For example, if you have $100,000 saved for real estate investment, it would be easy to get a good rental property that generates a monthly income of $800 with taxes and insurance costs excluded. Alternatively, you could scout for five such properties and approach a bank for a mortgage to finance the purchase of five rental properties. If you pay a 20% down payment on each property, the bank would lend you $80,000 for each property. Assuming the interest rate is 5% you would part with around $500 per month per property as payment inclusive of insurance and taxes. That means you are left with a rental income of $300 per property per month which translates to $1,500 from the 5 properties, which are more than double the rental income you could have generated from one property purchased without a debt. That is just an example of how you can use good debt to create wealth.

Wealth is freedom, it not only provides you with the resources to purchase wants but also gives you control over your life. Therefore, you should focus on building wealth with the aim of gaining financial freedom in the future. Sacrificing some of your wants when you are young makes it so you can enjoy the much-desired, yet rarely acquired financial freedom.

SAVING AND INVESTMENT APPS

Investing can seem intimidating and complicated, especially for beginners who do not know the ins and outs. You have learned how to stay out of debt and the best investment options for beginners, but how do you ensure that you stay on track and in the know about new investment opportunities? This is where technology comes in handy. Now that we all use smart mobile gadgets, it is easy to learn how to save and invest wisely with the help of investment apps.

Saving and investment apps are designed to help users save and invest in stocks or other assets based on their preferences from the palms of their hands. Different apps have different features but a core end goal: to help you, the user, make wiser and more informed investment decisions. All you need to get started is to install your preferred saving or investment app on your mobile device, add your primary bank details, choose an investment asset, buy shares, track your investment performance, and update and trade your portfolio as you deem fit. This way, you eliminate the need to pay an investment advisor or the time and resources you would have spent researching the best investment options. Here are a few saving and investment apps to get you started.

Acorns

Acorns is a micro-savings app that is designed to make saving and investing as easy as possible for beginners. The app rounds up spending to the nearest dollar and invests the difference for you. This way, investment feels painless because you only invest pennies at a time. You are required to link your checking and credit card accounts. Since the entire process of saving and investment account creation is created and managed on a smartphone, this app targets tech-savvy people, including the younger generation that tends to be less conversant with investing. It also makes it a great start for people who have never invested before or require investing guidance.

Acorns features a wide range of pre-made investment options that serve different types of investors. Apart from the spare change method, users can set up a recurring or one-time deposit method. Additionally, the app offers two types of investment accounts; Acorns Core and Acorns Later (an individual IRA account). Acorns Core charges $1 and Acorns Later charges $2 per month, while students with a .edu email address are granted access to the Acorns Core account free of charge for 4 years. You can also customize your account portfolio to be either conservative or aggressive.

Acorns implements the spare change transfers by monitoring your linked credit or debit account. For instance, if you spend $19.45 at the grocery store, the amount is rounded off to $20 and the extra 55 cents is added to your round-up balance. Once the rounded-up balance hits $5, it is withdrawn from your account and credited to your Acorns investment account. Note that you can choose the nature of transactions you want affected in the round-up feature or set it to automatic such that Acorns will round up all applicable expenses. You also have the option of turbo-charging the round-up amounts by up to ten times. In this case, instead of Acorns pitching the 55 cents from your store purchase, it invests $5.50. Another unique feature by Acorns is Found Money. With the Found Money feature, each time you use your Acorns-linked credit or debit card to pay for a product or services at a partner retailer, the retailer contributes an extra amount to your Acorns account.

Stash

The Stash investment app aims to make the selection of exchange-traded funds and stocks investment easy and quick for beginners. For a $1 monthly fee, you gain access to the brokerage account, Stash online bank account, a debit card, and a rewards program. For $3 per month, you are offered a brokerage account, a bank account, and a retirement investment account like the traditional IRA or Roth. For $9 per month, you are granted all the aforementioned features and, in addition, two custodial accounts for minors, a turbocharged reward program, an investment research report every month, and a metallic debit card. On the bright side, the minimum account balance is $0 and the app offers fractional investment options. As such, you can buy portions of fund share or stock from a company for pennies. With such features, Stash is ideal for novice investors, investors who need guidance, and impact investors.

The main aim of the Stash app is to help beginners to learn how to invest. To ensure that the app prioritizes your preferred and ideal investment options, the app asks new account subscribers a few questions, then gives a list of ETFs narrowed down to those ideal for you based on your financial goals and risk tolerance. The app highlights the best investment options that should serve as your portfolio foundation and those that are ideal as portfolio complements. Given this information, it is upon you to build an investment portfolio you deem appropriate. However, should the Stash Coach feature notice a lack of diversification in your investment options, it nudges back and offers additional investment education content to ensure that you make the right choices.

In addition, the Stash Portfolio Builder offers a list of ETFs representing a diverse investment portfolio. You are allowed to invest in the portfolio, or to add or remove investments as you wish. Though such portfolios are built out of ETFs, the app also offers individual stock investment options. As a matter of fact, the app features more than 1800 stocks and ETFs, including the Costco and Apple stocks. With the app's Fractional Shares feature, you can own a part of a company whose share price is high with just $1 investment.

For both individual stocks and ETF investment options, the app offers information like a quick and detailed synopsis of what the investment entails, bar visualization that acts as the risk level representation, ticker symbol, last stock price, and expense ratio for ETFs. ETF descriptions include a list of investment holdings and underlying security. With such information, you can confidently make an investment without fear of the unknown. Unlike most apps, stash offers a social component that allows users to connect with other app investors with similar risk profiles through Facebook or other contact methods of choice. An app's section is dedicated to provision of investment information that varies based on a user's investment preferences and risk tolerance.

TD Ameritrade

TD Ameritrade is an app by the renowned brokerage firm TD Ameritrade. The mobile app is ideal for investors who seek detailed and extensive information about stocks, markets and companies. It provides a series of informative videos that are designed to teach users about the different stock investment strategies based on market volatility and their risk tolerance levels. The minimum required deposit is $0 and the app has over 300 in-person customer support branches. Based on the nature of investment information and trading platforms it provides, TD Ameritrade is ideal for beginners, advanced investors, fund investors, commission-free traders and people in need of factual and extensive investment education.

The unique feature offered by TD Ameritrade is its virtual trading simulator, which acts as a mock trading account. The virtual trading simulator is a desktop optimized platform that is ideal for frequent and advanced traders. Initially, users are offered $100,000 virtual trading money and margin account access. Note that non-users are allowed to register for a free 60-day trial period, which is a great way to test a new investment platform before committing your resources and time.

Summary

Savings and investment apps are designed with the intent of cultivating an investing culture by making required resources accessible to people in a convenient manner as the internet of things takes shape. However, though the apps provide detailed and factual investment information, some investment lingo and strategies may be hard to decipher, especially for beginners. In such a case, it is advisable to seek guidance from a financial advisor and resume the use of apps once you understand the basic investment terminologies and strategies.

Chapter Summary

- You do not need a lot of money to start your wealth-building journey.
- Start building wealth while you are still young to reap maximum benefits from compounded interest in the future and more so, after retirement.
- Anyone can invest in real estate, but it takes time

to learn the market strategies and become a top-rated investor.
- It is important to diversify your investment portfolios in order to mitigate risks and possible losses.

FINAL WORDS

Debt can drive you into financial slavery by limiting your freedom and ability to enjoy life. We often find ourselves trapped in debt without even realizing how it happened. You simply take a small debt in confidence that you will pay it off in time, but before you pay it off, you take on another small debt. Before you know it, you are in huge debt and do not even know where to start to dig yourself out of it. This is the sad financial state of many Americans, who, in many cases, take on debt trying to "keep up with the Joneses." But, if people would live within their means, stay out of debt, and focus on creating wealth instead, they would surpass the Joneses and live their best life without worrying about debt or running out of cash.

As you have learned from this book, there is always a price to pay for bad financial decisions. You may enjoy instant gratification from acquiring that designer watch, shoes, a new car, or the latest phone, but you will struggle in silence as you pay down the high-interest debt. As explained, there are sweeter fruits to enjoy in the future if you forego wants for needs now. For starters, you should forego some of those wants to pay off debt. Eventually, it will be easier to make sacrifices, save, and invest in wealth building ventures like real estate, bonds, stock markets, or entrepreneurship.

Above all, it is important to always work around a budget and be financially disciplined. You can be sure that it takes time and sacrifice to get out of debt. Moreover, the emotional and mental stress that comes from carrying a lot of debt is not worth experiencing. It is up to you to work towards securing your financial future and avoid falling back into debt. Start by building an emergency fund. You should have at least six months of your income before you venture into investments. Embrace goal-oriented saving in order to remain motivated and disciplined not to divert the money. Financial organization is key!

As you focus on taking out good debt to build your net worth and secure your financial future, it is also important to keep learning and researching new and profitable investment ideas. The economy changes daily, and that translates to new investment opportunities that you can cash in on. As the saying goes, the early bird catches the worm. Educate yourself on personal finance by reading finance books, following top-rated investors on social media, and when possible by attending personal finance and investment webinars. There is always something new to learn about personal finance, building wealth, and investments. Most importantly, associate with like-minded people who are focused on creating wealth and acquiring financial freedom; their spending habits are different and they will always have something new to offer.

Lastly, if you loved the content in this book and if it has been helpful to you, I would sincerely appreciate it if you would consider leaving a positive review for it online.

OTHER BOOKS BY MICHAEL STEVEN
Financial Freedom With Real Estate

Start Making Money Today Because Everyone Else Is

[3 Simple Ways that Even Your Kids Can Do It: Secrets Guaranteed to Work Right Away]

VISIT my website to see my new books and to follow me on Social Media.

www.thebestsellerbooks.com

FINANCIAL FREEDOM CHECKLIST

(A Simple list that should be followed to the "T")

This checklist includes:

❏ 11 important steps that you should follow to achieve success and head toward *Financial Freedom.*

❏ Plus, bonus advice.

Forget about yesterday and start thinking about tomorrow!

"The past and the future are separated by a second,

so make that second count!"

—Carmine Pirone

To receive your Financial Freedom With Real Estate checklist, visit the link:

www.thebestsellerbooks.com

ADDITIONAL RESOURCE

Laws that protect you when you are in debt

We all take out debt with the confidence that we will pay it off as agreed upon with the lender. But, sometimes financial calamity strikes and we are not able to honor our end of the bargain. Unfortunately, debt collectors do not always understand and they are known to use force or threats to coerce debtors to clear debts. The good news is that the law protects debtors from such harassment from debt collectors.

The Fair Debt Collection Practices Act protects debtors against harassment that includes abusive language, threats of harm, arrest or violence, and excessive phone calls. It gives debtors the right to seek proof that they indeed owe the debt collectors the amount of money they demand. It prohibits debt collectors from disclosing debts to unauthorized third parties. Contacting debtors during inconvenient hours like before 8 am and after 9 pm is prohibited. Conversely, it gives debtors the right to sue debt collectors for violation of any of these provisions.

Moreover, debt collectors are required to contact debtors in writing about their outstanding debt and arrears. The debt collection notice should contain information such as the debt collector's name and address, outstanding debt amount clearly indicating the principal amount, interest and penalties where applicable, the lender's name, and a statement that failure to dispute the debt within 30 days will deem the debt valid among other things. Should a debt collector call, they should first verify that you are the rightful debtor before disclosing any information about the debt. They should also give information about their company upon request.

Unfortunately, most people are not aware of such fair debt collection laws that protect them from harassment and humiliation by debt collectors. If you feel harassed by a debt collector, it would be wise to seek legal advice and if things get out of hand, you should consider suing the debt collector for harassment.

Lastly, if you loved the content in this book and if it has been helpful to you, I would sincerely appreciate it if you would consider leaving a positive review for it online.

REFERENCES

1. Megan Leonhardt, Federal lawmakers aim to reduce payday loan rates from 400% interest to 36%, https://www.cnbc.com/2019/11/12/federal-lawmakers-look-to-take-payday-loan-rates-from-400-percent-to-36-percent.html

2. Kyoung et al, Poverty levels and debt indicators among low-income households before and after the great recession, https://files.eric.ed.gov/fulltext/EJ1162059.pdf

3. Zack Friedman, 78% of workers live paycheck to paycheck, https://www.forbes.com/sites/zackfriedman/2019/01/11/live-paycheck-to-paycheck-government-shutdown/#2961abd4f10b

4. The Aspen Institute, Consumer debt, https://assets.aspeninstitute.org/content/uploads/2018/03/ASPEN_ConsumerDebt_06B.pdf

5. Anya Bennet, 7 causes people get into debt, https://www.lifehack.org/articles/money/7-causes-people-get-into-debt.html

6. Bill Fay, The emotional effects of debt, https://www.debt.org/advice/emotional-effects/

7. Miriam Caldwell, How to improve your financial situation, https://www.thebalance.com/plan-to-turn-around-your-finances-4119172

8. David Haynes, How to negotiate with creditors and settle your debt, https://www.thebalance.com/how-to-negotiate-with-your-creditors-316120

9. Martin Dasko, Where you stand financially, https://financialhighway.com/where-do-you-stand-financially/

10. Valencia Higuera, Emotional effects of having too much debt

and how to cope, https://www.moneycrashers.com/emotional-effects-debt-cope/

11. Bill Fay, Key figures behind America's consumer debt, https://www.debt.org/faqs/americans-in-debt/

12. Justin Pritchard, Escape the debt cycle, https://www.thebalance.com/get-out-of-the-debt-cycle-4054269

13. Ben Le Fort, Ranking the 7 types of debt from worst to best, https://medium.com/makingofamillionaire/ranking-the-6-types-of-debt-from-worst-to-best-3788f01b86e3

14. Bill Fay, Good debt vs. bad debt, https://www.debt.org/advice/good-vs-bad/

15. Jeff Rose, 9 ways to build wealth fast(that your financial advisor might not tell you), https://www.forbes.com/sites/jrose/2019/09/26/ways-to-build-wealth-fast-that-your-financial-advisor-wont-tell-you/#2df419c67401

16. The Oracles, Real estate is still the best investment you can make today, millionaires say – here's why, https://www.cnbc.com/2019/10/01/real-estate-is-still-the-best-investment-you-can-make-today-millionaires-say.html

17. Brianna McGurran & Arielle O'Shea, How to start investing: A guide for beginners, https://www.nerdwallet.com/article/investing/how-to-start-investing

18. U.S. Bank | U.S. Bancorp Investments, Good debt: Using debt to build wealth, https://financialiq.usbank.com/index/manage-your-household/manage-debt/good-debt-using-debt-to-build-wealth.html

19. Credit.com, 20 ways to stay out of debt, https://clark.com/personal-finance-credit/ways-to-stay-out-of-debt/

20. Chonce Maddox, Change your habits, stay out of debt, https://www.moneyunder30.com/change-habits-stay-out-of-debt

21. Annie Nova, How to buy a car, with less debt, https://www.cnbc.com/2018/12/31/how-to-buy-a-car-with-less-debt.html

22. Robert Farrington, 5 alternative ways to pay for college, https://www.forbes.com/sites/robertfarrington/2020/03/11/5-alternative-ways-to-pay-for-college/#58bc82001195

23. Carolyn Steber, Experts reveal how to avoid going into debt when you're planning your wedding, https://www.bustle.com/p/how-to-avoid-going-into-debt-for-your-wedding-according-to-experts-18797944

24. Consumer-action.org, Debtor's rights, https://www.bustle.com/p/how-to-avoid-going-into-debt-for-your-wedding-according-to-experts-18797944

Printed in Great Britain
by Amazon

Pen to Published

A 6-month programme that will enable you to write, publish and promote your book
with Amazon bestselling author Shalini Bhalla-Lucas

You know you have a book in you.
You just don't know how to get it out there…
Let me show you how.

With my Zoom programme you will be able to get your ideas down on paper and be published online on Amazon in SIX months. The programme will keep you focused and accountable – which is what you need when you want to successfully write, publish and promote your book.

This is the first time I have been part of a book writing course. I have learned so much from Shalini about how to structure a book by incorporating different writing style approaches and techniques. I am so pleased with the level of support, help and guidance received and would highly recommend "Pen to Published" to anyone who is thinking about writing a book. **Joti Gata-Aura, London**

I have started writing a book many times, but lacked the time and motivation to get past a couple of chapters. "Pen to Published" gave me the structure and accountability I needed, plus incredible support from Shalini and her knowledge around writing, formatting, editing and publishing. I set out with the aim to come out of lockdown as an author and I achieved it! **Ami Lauren, Devon**

For more information about Pen to Published please email info@justjhoom.co.uk **or visit** www.justjhoom.co.uk

About the Author

A qualified safari guide, environmental scientist and science communicator, Rosie Miles works as a wildlife researcher and conservationist in Southern Africa.

Having grown up in the United Kingdom and studied in New Zealand, Rosie moved to South Africa in 2010 to follow a decade-long dream to become a safari guide.

Combining her guiding knowledge with her scientific background, she found the perfect place to put her unique set of skills to use, managing wildlife conservation projects across Africa. She is currently based in Malawi.

In 2019, she completed a post graduate degree in Science Communications, and is passionate about sharing her knowledge on wildlife and conservation through a range of channels.

Girl of the Wild is Rosie's first book.

For more information about Rosie and her adventures in the wild follow her on Instagram: @safari_smiles

Note from the Author

The stories in this book are true, however are recounted from my memory and are therefore subjective and inherently biased. The experiences and conversations may be remembered differently by those involved. Other than where I have abbreviated events to improve readability, any other discrepancies that do exist between my own and other people's viewpoints are not intentional. I have made every attempt to retain the accuracy of the narrative according to my memory of the events.

I have deliberately refrained from using the names of people and places to protect their identities. If, despite this, I have inadvertently caused any offence, hurt or distress to anyone then I give my sincere apologies.

Finally, I want to thank everyone who has ever told me to write this book. I hope you will enjoy reading it as much as I have enjoyed writing it.

Long-time friend and fellow guide, Andreas Fox, an excellent writer in his own right, gave invaluable editing feedback and provided expert advice on the wildlife anecdotes. But beyond that Andreas has always been one of my biggest motivators, believing in me more than I ever could, and for that I am forever grateful. Finally, Emma Brisdion, a science communications guru, has been my sounding board throughout this process and I have greatly valued your thoughts and advice.

It is always a pleasure working with Stuart Kinlough, who designed the cover for this book. He somehow manages to tap into the inner workings of my brain, even when I am unable to articulate what I am imagining, and then produces something beautiful out of it.

Most importantly, I would like to thank Shalini Bhalla-Lucas for her expert guidance during this writing process, as well as the support and friendship from the other ladies with whom I have been on this book writing journey with as part of Shalini's Pen to Published course. I met Shalini when I hitched a ride with her to Nairobi following a conference we had both been attending in Limuru, Kenya. During the hour-long drive back to the city we bonded over a mutual love of dancing, cricket and writing, and remained in contact ever since. When, months later, she asked if I would like to be a part of the Pen to Published course for first-time writers, I didn't hesitate for a second. During the challenging times that the Covid-19 pandemic has brought, the process of writing this book has been cathartic and more fun than I ever imagined I could have sitting in front of a laptop. So, thank you Shalini for providing me with this opportunity.

Acknowledgements

First of all, I must thank my family who have not only supported, but actively encouraged, all of my life choices regardless of how unexpected or wild they are. Without their unwavering belief that there are no limits in life, I never would have embarked on this journey in the first place.

I would also like to thank them, and my friends, who graciously put up with me turning up on the doorstep with a carload of my worldly possessions every time I am temporarily homeless from my nomadic adventures. Not least Victoria Cooke, who, not only frequently has a spare room full of my belongings, but who also has an exceptional talent to tame my unruly locks whenever I need to look a little less wild.

To the people who have been a part of all the extraordinary experiences over the years, including those I couldn't fit in this book, there are too many of you to mention, but you know who you are. It wouldn't have been the same without you. An especially big shout-out to all my girls of the wild who have each other's backs through thick and thin and never give up on the dream.

A special thanks to my fantastic support crew and team of editors who have helped get this book into a publishable state. Each bringing their own skills and expertise to the task, I feel lucky to have been able to bring you on board. My uncle Nigel Nelson, who himself wrote a children's book featuring me as a main character after I complained that all the Rosie's in books were pigs or hippos and never little girls. I knew I could rely on you to scrutinize my writing to a professional standard.

Chapter 9

[11] Anthony, Marc. The Beautiful Truth. Createspace Independent Publishing Platform. 2016

Chapter 10

[12] Rowe, Nikki. Nikki Rowe Quotes. Goodreads.com. Goodreads, Inc. 2021. https://www.goodreads.com/quotes/10085486-a-warrior-still-needs-love-and-affection-the-same-way (online - accessed 26 March 2021)

Chapter 11

[13] Melody, Lee. Moon Gypsy. A Collection of Poetry and Prose. Createspace Independent Publishing Platform. 2017

Epilogue

[14] Usher, David. Let the Elephants Run: Unlock Your Creativity and Change Everything. House of Anansi Press; 1st Edition. 2015

[15] Drake, Robert M. Broken Flowers. Andrews McMeel Publishing. 2016

Photo and Design Credits

Cover Design by Stuart Kinlough: www.stuartkinlough.co.uk

Author Photograph by Victoria Cooke

[6] Word, J. Iron. J. Iron Word Quotes. Goodreads inc. 2021. https://www.goodreads.com/author/quotes/15037995.J_Iron_Word (online - accessed 26 March 2021)

Chapter 5

[7] Rowe, Nikki. Nikki Rowe Quotes. Goodreads.com. Goodreads, Inc. 2021.https://www.goodreads.com/quotes/8114731-some-are-born-to-play-it-safe-others-are-born (online - accessed 26 March 2021)

Chapter 6

[8] Aspen, Matis. Girl in the Woods: A Memoir. William Morrow. 2015

Chapter 7

[9] Rowe, Nikki. Nikki Rowe Quotes. Goodreads.com. Goodreads, Inc. 2021.https://www.goodreads.com/quotes/7676384-she-was-wild-and-free-with-a-dab-of-logic (online - accessed 26 March 2021)

Chapter 8

[10] Gill, Nikita. Girls of the Wild. Meanwhile:Poetry. Tumbler. https://meanwhilepoetry.tumblr.com/post/151529465803/they-wont-tell-you-fairytales-of-how-girls-can-be (online - accessed 26 March 2021)

Quote Credits

Every effort has been made to correctly credit the quote sources, but if any have been inadvertently overlooked or incorrectly referenced, please contact the publishers or the author.

[1] Gill, Nikita. Fierce Fairytales: & Other Stories to Stir Your Soul. Trapeze. 2018

Introduction

[2] Gillman, Michelle Rose. Bella Grace: Life's A Beautiful Journey 2021. Issue 26. Stampington & Company. 2021

Chapter 1

[3] Rowe, Nikki. Nikki Rowe Quotes. Goodreads.com. Goodreads, Inc. 2021. https://www.goodreads.com/quotes/7490078-and-then-she-learnt-to-be-a-little-wild-she (online - accessed 26 March 2021)

Chapter 2

[4] Gill, Nikita. The Girl and the Goddess. Ebury Press. 2020

Chapter 3

[5] Wilson, Heidi. *Heidi Wilson: Quotes of the Week. BellaGraceMagazine.com, Stampington & Company. 2021. https://bellagracemagazine.com/quotes-of-the-week/ (online - accessed 26 March 2021)*

Chapter 4